Benton Mennonite Church
15350 County Road 44
Goshen, Indiana 46528

Earth **trek**

Earth trek

Celebrating and sustaining God's creation

Joanne Moyer
Commissioned by Mennonite Central Committee

Herald
Press

Waterloo, Ontario
Scottdale, Pennsylvania

Library and Archives Canada Cataloguing in Publication

Moyer, Joanne, 1978-

Earth trek : celebrating and sustaining God's creation / Joanne Moyer ; commissioned by Mennonite Central Committee.

ISBN 0-8361-9291-5

1. Human ecology--Religious aspects--Christianity. 2. Environmental ethics. 3. Nature--Religious aspects--Christianity.

I. Mennonite Central Committee. II. Title.

BT695.5.M69 2004 241'.691

C2004-905175-X

Scripture quotations are from the New Revised Standard Version, copyright ©1989, by the Division of Christian Education of the National Council of the Churches of Christ in the USA, and is used by permission.

EARTH TREK

Copyright © 2004 by Herald Press, Scottdale, Pa. 15683

Published simultaneously in Canada by Herald Press,

Waterloo, Ont. N2L 6H7. All rights reserved

Canadian Entry Number: C2004-905175-X

Library of Congress Control Number: 2004112704

International Standard Book Number: 0-8361-9291-5

Printed in the United States of America

Book and cover design by Roberta Fast

10 09 08 07 06 05 04 10 9 8 7 6 5 4 3 2 1

To order or request information, please call
1-800-759-4447 (individuals); 1-800-245-7894 (trade).
Website: www.heraldpress.com

To my parents, Beth and Jim,
for teaching me to love creation and the Creator,
and to my sister, Marie,
for laughter and inspiration.

it is still good

(An adaptation of Genesis 1)

In the beginning when God created the heavens and the earth, the earth was formless and void and darkness covered the face of the deep while a wind from God swept over the face of the waters.

Then God said, "Let there be light," and there was light. And God saw that the light was good; and God separated the light from the darkness. God called the light Day, and the darkness God called Night. And there was evening and there was morning.
The first day.

And God said, "Let there be a dome in the midst of the waters, and let it separate the water from the waters."
The second day.

And God said, "Let the waters under the sky be gathered together into one place, and let the dry land appear." Then God said, "Let the earth put forth vegetation, plants yield- ing seed, and fruit trees bearing fruit in which is their seed, each according to its kind, upon the earth." And it was good.
The third day.

And God said, "Let there be lights in the sky to separate the day from the night."
The fourth day.

And God said, "Let the waters bring forth swarms of living creatures, and let birds fly above the earth across the sky." And God blessed them, saying, "Be fruitful and multi- ply and fill the waters in the seas, and let birds multiply on the earth."
The fifth day.

And God said, "Let the earth bring forth living creatures according to every kind: cattle and creeping things and wild animals of every kind." And God saw that it was good.

It was good: the light, the sky, the land, the waters were good. The plants, the fish, the birds, the animals were good. But creation was not complete.

Then God said, "Let us make humankind in our image, after our likeness; and let them have dominion over all the earth." So God created humankind in his image, male and female God created them. God blessed them, and God said to them, "Be fruitful and multiply, and fill the earth and subdue it. Have dominion over the fish of the sea and over the birds of the air and over every living thing that moves upon the earth."
The sixth day.

But what has happened since we who were created in the image of God have taken dominion over all the earth?

The balance in the heavens is being disturbed and good light is becoming a menace. Good skies are being choked with toxic fumes. Good lands are losing their nutrients. And good waters are being poisoned.

Good forests are disappearing. Good creatures of the sea are vanishing. Good birds are being exterminated for sport. And good animals are losing their homes in the wild.

When God sees everything God has made, and what we who were created in God's image have done, is it still good?

God saw everything that God had made, and indeed, it was very good.

Though we may maim, destroy and pollute, we cannot remove the goodness of what God has made. Nor can we escape our calling as creatures made in God's image: to live peaceably on God's good Earth.

introduction

In the beginning God created the heavens and the earth and God saw that the creation was good. It is still good. As children of the Creator and followers of his Son, Christians are called to celebrate the good creation and to strive to sustain it.

e*arth trek* sets about the task of celebrating and sustaining the Earth by embarking on a journey of discovery into the intricacies of this creation in which we live. The purpose of the journey is to learn to better understand creation and our place within it, and to move us to action.

A deeper understanding enables celebration of the Earth in the same way that a relationship with a friend becomes more cherished the better the friend is known. In the words of theologian Sallie McFague, "we must pay attention—detailed, careful, concrete attention—to the world that lies around us but is not us. We must do this because we cannot love what we do not know." Celebration also occurs through worship and through theological reflection.

A deeper understanding of the creation and our place in it also contributes to sustaining the Earth because it is only with an understanding of how creation works and flows that it is possible to live peaceably within those patterns. In addition, theological reflection helps to integrate creation care into our understanding of discipleship.

The *Earth trek* is structured around the Genesis 1 story of creation, using each "day" as a starting point for examining the elements of creation. Each "day" includes two to six sessions containing four sections: Earth Connection, Faith Connection, For Meditation, and For Action. The Earth Connection examines how the elements of creation are being threatened or redeemed. The Faith Connection delves into the Christian faith tradition and what it teaches about how God and humankind relate to the Earth and its creatures. For Meditation provides prayers and quotations for reflection and worship. Finally, For Action lists action suggestions which you are encouraged to introduce into your daily life. These suggestions reflect a broad range of possibilities recognizing that there are many ways to achieve sustainability and that people in different situations and stages in life have different needs and capabilities. Some actions are very simple while others are more challenging and profoundly transformative. Begin with those actions that are the easiest to fit into your life and work up to those that are more challenging.

Earth trek material was originally developed for a Mennonite Central Committee (MCC) Web site, entitled "7-Days—It is still good: An Earth Care Trek for Christians." In its book form, it can be used for personal meditation and reflection, for group study and discernment, and as a resource for worship and action. Individuals or groups may wish to work through the book over a period of time, doing one session per week (as it was presented on the web site) or perhaps one "day" per month. Individuals may wish to work through the material by journalling, while groups can use it as a starting point for discussion. Groups can also serve as a place for encouragement and accountability for integrating the action suggestions into the daily lives of the group members.

The health of the planet Earth and the human responsibility for its ills are increasingly urgent issues in our world. Creation sustains every aspect of our lives and the lives of everything we cherish, and yet, it is being systematically degraded and destroyed. Many people are unaware of how profoundly their actions affect the health of creation and how urgently the Earth's diseases need to be treated. Those who are aware of the problem often feel overwhelmed and do not know what to do. *Earth trek* endeavours to address this situation.

As you embark on this trek, I invite you to do so joyfully. There are many grievous stories to be told about the state of the Earth, and the actions necessary to remedy these situations are sometimes hard. But even as we mourn the degradation of the good creation, we can celebrate that it was made and be encouraged that the Creator has not abandoned creation. By walking the path toward greater sustainability with the Earth, we are walking the path of the kingdom of God. May God bless you on your journey.

in the beginning . . .

 # in the beginning

"Just to be is a blessing; just to live is holy."—Abraham Heschel

earth trek begins with a survey of general issues and ideas that will serve as a foundation for the journey. This includes introducing some fundamental concepts of ecology and the basic relationship between Christian faith and creation, and exploring both the practical and spiritual reasons for caring for creation.

> *"In the beginning when God created the heavens and the earth, the earth was a formless void and darkness covered the face of the deep, while a wind from God swept over the face of the waters."*
> *—Genesis 1:1-2*

WEEK 1
earth connection the living earth

The natural world is composed of a complex mix of energy, matter, and life which forms the physical aspects of our planet and support the living creatures that reside here. Energy, matter and life interact to maintain a balance which allows the Earth to survive and prosper.

The Earth has a phenomenal ability to maintain this balance, but it can be destroyed. If the natural mechanisms by which the Earth sustains itself are disrupted, all the interconnected pieces will suffer.

Human beings are members of the life community of the planet, and like other living creatures we depend on the natural processes of the Earth to support our lives. At the same time, we have the power to alter aspects of these systems and thus we can disrupt the stability and integrity of the entire planet. This puts all of creation in jeopardy. As members of the Earth community, it is important that we understand both how the system we depend on functions and our power to interfere with it. Energy, matter and life systems, and the roles they play on the planet.

energy: Energy drives everything on the planet. Most energy enters the Earth system as radiation from the sun and flows through both the physical environment and all that lives on the Earth. Through this process it is converted into different forms. These forms include chemical energy, such as the energy stored in food; mechanical energy, which is the energy in moving objects; and heat. With each conversion, some usable energy is lost as heat. Energy cannot be created or destroyed.

m a t t e r : The nonliving, or abiotic, components of the environment can be divided into three spheres: the atmosphere, the hydrosphere, and the lithosphere.

- The atmosphere is the gaseous envelope that surrounds the Earth, consisting of air, vapour, and small particles.
- The hydrosphere includes all the waters on and around the Earth.
- The lithosphere consists of the outer surface and interior of the solid earth, and is composed of rocks, minerals, and elements. Like energy, the basic elements of matter cannot be created or destroyed, but instead go through cycles. Examples of these cycles are the water cycle, the carbon cycle, and the nitrogen cycle.

l i f e : The component of the planet that includes all living things is called the biosphere. Living organisms can be categorized according to how they obtain energy.

- Producers, which are mostly plants, convert sunlight into chemical energy through photosynthesis.
- Consumers obtain their energy from other organisms on which they feed. They can be divided into herbivores, which eat plants; carnivores, which eat animals; and omnivores, which eat both plants and animals.
- Decomposers, like consumers, obtain their energy from other organisms, but feed exclusively on dead organic material. In the process, decomposers, such as bacteria and fungi, help break matter down so it can return to the abiotic environment. The interaction between producers, consumers, and decomposers is often described as the food chain, the food pyramid, or the food web.

Energy, matter, and life combine together into a complex set of relationships called an ecosystem. Ecosystems consist of all the different species of life that share a specific physical area, and are defined by the interactions between those living species and their abiotic environment. Ecosystem are healthy when all their component parts—matter and energy, living, and nonliving—exist in proper balance.

FOR DISCUSSION AND REFLECTION

With all our technology, many humans live our lives removed from nature. Yet we are still members of the Earth community. What place do humans fill in the natural world? How do we fit into the natural processes described above?

faith connection christianity and creation

The following principles are a summary of biblical teachings relating to creation and the place of humankind within it. These principles form the basis for the Faith Connection discussions which follow.

God loves all creation.

God delights in creation and cares for the well-being of all creatures (Gen. 1).

creation reveals God's character.

Through creation itself, God's character can be seen (Rom. 1:19-20) and all things created give praise to God (Ps. 19:1-6; Ps. 148). Wilderness places facilitate close encounters with God (Exod. 3:1-2) and provide a place of testing and retreat (Mark 1:12-13).

creation belongs to God.

"The earth is the Lord's and all that is in it" (Ps. 24:1). God is sovereign over the Earth and everything it produces is a gift from God. It is through God's grace, and not human effort, that the Earth is fertile and supports life.

human beings are an inseparable part of God's creation.

Human kinship with creation is expressed in Genesis when God forms Adam from the dust of the ground (Gen. 2:7). Human beings also share their day of creation with the animals (Gen. 1:24-30). This highlights our dependence on and connectedness to creation.

human beings have a special role and responsibility within creation.

Human beings were made in the image of God (Gen. 1:26-27). This gives us a position both of privilege and of responsibility within creation. Our role can be understood as stewardship: serving creation under the ultimate rule of God.

a moral relationship exists between humans and creation.

Creation is affected by human action. God blesses human faithfulness by causing the Earth to flourish (Deut. 28:1-6), and uses the forces of nature to punish human sin (Jer. 14:1-10). Decay and destruction of the natural world is often a consequence of human sin.

God's plan of salvation includes the restoration of creation.

Biblical visions of renewal and restoration include creation. Redemption causes the Earth to produce bountiful gifts (Amos 9:13), the lion to lie down with the lamb (Isa. 11:6-9), and a new heaven and a new earth to be made (Rev. 21:1).

Jesus plays a role in both creating and restoring creation.

Jesus is the first-born of all creation and participates in the creation of the world (Col. 1:15-16). As such, Jesus has authority over creation (Luke 8:22-25), and its restoration is encompassed in the salvation that he brings.

Jesus cares for creation.

Through his teaching, his simple lifestyle, his concern for the weak and the poor (Matt. 5:3-11), and his attitude of service and humility (Phil. 2:6-8), Jesus demonstrates care for creation and exemplifies a creation-friendly way to live. *(Adapted from William van Geest)*

FOR DISCUSSION AND REFLECTION

What do you think of the above discussion of Christianity and creation? Does it fit into your understanding of Christianity? Why is it important for Christians to articulate a caring response to the environment?

for meditation

"Help us be gentle with your creatures and handiwork so that we may abide in your eternal salvation and continue to be held in the hollow of your hand."
—An Amish Prayer

for action

keep a nature journal noting your observations of the natural world each day.

look in your pockets, purse, or bag to find something that symbolizes or represents a personal action that you are taking toward the environment. Do this activity as a group.

look at your favourite hymns, choruses, or Bible verses what do they say about creation? Do this activity as a group.

Learn about the **environmental issues** in your area.

Learn about the **environmental groups** that are working in your area:

Canadian Environmental Network **www.cen-rce.org**

Environment Canada **www.ec.gc.ca**

Environmental Protection Agency (USA) **www.epa.gov**

Read the Evangelical Declaration on the Care of Creation **www.creationcare.org/resources/declaration.php**

Read the Catholic Declaration on the Environment **http://conservation.catholic.org/declaration.htm**

say a prayer of thanks-giving each day this week for aspects of nature that touch your life.

WEEK 2
earth connection the land ethic

"A thing is right when it tends to preserve the integrity, stability, and beauty of the biotic [living] community. It is wrong when it tends otherwise."—Aldo Leopold

The "land ethic" was introduced by Aldo Leopold, an American forester and ecologist during the early twentieth century. He contributed significantly to conservation and the transformation of attitudes toward nature in North America by suggesting that the land is worthy of moral consideration. Up to that point, it was generally accepted in western society that human beings only had moral responsibilities toward other humans. Animals, plants, minerals, rivers, and oceans were there to be dominated, tamed, and exploited for human use and enjoyment. They had no worth or value outside their usefulness to people.

Leopold challenged this premise by arguing that "the land," meaning soils, waters, plants, and animals, have intrinsic value—value which is completely separate from their usefulness to human beings. This argument developed from his growing understanding of the complexity and interrelatedness of the natural world. All the pieces play a part in the larger whole and therefore have a worth and value in their very existence. Based on this new premise, Leopold presented the land ethic as the measure for guiding human interactions with the land.

"We abuse the land because we regard it as a commodity belonging to us. When we see the land as a community to which we belong, we may begin to use it with love and respect."—Aldo Leopold

faith connection

The natural world provides a great range of services necessary for human survival, but creation's value extends beyond its use to us: it is full of beauty, wonder, and joy. The conclusions that Aldo Leopold reached about the value of the land through studying ecology can also be found by reflecting on the biblical story. The Genesis 1 account of creation is permeated with expressions of God's pleasure and satisfaction in creation, and the artistry and care with which God infused the world are obvious when we look around us. Creation has intrinsic value because it was created by God and God declared it good.

"The cosmos, in all its beauty, wildness, and life-giving bounty, is the work of our personal and loving Creator . . . The Creator's concern is for all creatures. God declares all creation 'good' (Gen. 1:31); promises care in a covenant with all creatures (Gen. 9:9–17); delights in creatures which have no human apparent usefulness (Job 39–41); and wills, in Christ, 'to reconcile all things to himself' (Col. 1:20)."—Evangelical declaration on the care of creation

FOR DISCUSSION AND REFLECTION

Both the church and secular culture sometimes teach that the world was created for humans alone. Do you agree? Why or why not?

for meditation

All things by immortal power,
Near or far,
Hiddenly
To each other linked are,
That thou canst not stir a flower
Without troubling of a star.

—Francis Thompson

for action

read Genesis 1; say a prayer of thanks to God.

As you travel through the Trek, **write or draw ideas** for creation care actions on recipe cards, put them into a photo album, and make the album accessible to other people (in a church, community centre, etc.). Encourage others to add to the album.

Find out what **natural plants and animals** live in your neighbourhood or region.

**make
creation care
the theme**
of a group retreat or
camping trip.

**plan a
worship service**
about creation
care for your
congregation.

**visit a
"wild" place**
near you. Reflect on
its value apart
from your use
of it.

**attune
your senses**
to the world around
you. What does your
neighbourhood smell,
sound, look, and
feel like?

**take
a walk** in the
neighbourhood around
your home or church and
note what is natural
and what is
human-made.

God at play

Oct. 23 / 2003: 4:30 a.m.

I am standing on a low point of land which juts into the Manigotogan River
north of Winnipeg. The sweet smoke of a hardwood fire permeates the night
air. In the old log cabin at my back, friends slumber in the arms of an impene-
trable silence. A silver sliver of moon hangs low in the eastern sky. Orion
burns clear as headlights to the south, reflecting on the rippled river. To the
north, the west, and directly overhead flashing, swirling, and streaking
Northern Lights. Aurora Borealis; God at play. "Oh, you liked that one? Watch
this."—*7-Days trek participant*

let there be light . . .

 Day 1: **let there be light**

"The sun and the moon and the stars would have disappeared long ago . . .
had they happened to be within the reach of predatory human hands."
—Havelock Ellis

energy pervades all of life and activity on the Earth and is vital to the functioning of all human endeavours. In today's industrialized and technological world, the human appetite for energy has become insatiable. We tear up forests, mountains and the ocean floor to extract it, and we probably would draw it from the moon and the stars if we could. Day 1 looks at social and environmental aspects of finding and using energy. It also explores how the spirit of God, like energy, pervades all of creation and how creation is thereby a revelation of God's character.

"Then God said, 'Let there be light,' and there was light.
And God saw the light was good; and God separated
the light from the darkness. God called the light Day, and the
darkness he called Night. And there was evening and
there was morning, the first day."
—Genesis 1:3-5

WEEK 1
earth connection

Shortly after 4:00 p.m. on August 14, 2003, a major power outage hit most of Ontario and much of the northeastern United States. The lights went out, computers shut down, and air conditioners turned off. Without traffic lights, cars slowed to a crawl, and stalled subway systems filled the streets with pedestrians. People were trapped in elevators and those who couldn't navigate stairs were stuck in tall buildings. As fridges and freezers warmed and electric ranges sat idle, food began to go bad and long lines formed at hot dog stands. The power outage even disrupted airline traffic, stranding travelers across the country.

Events like the 2003 power outage remind us how dependent we are on electricity, one of the most common forms of energy used in industrialized societies. Energy is vital to our lives, but the conveniences and luxuries many of us enjoy require immense expenditures of the Earth's resources. And improving the standard of living for people in less developed countries will require even more.

While there are immense reserves of energy in the natural world, particularly in the sun, the challenge is finding ways to harness that energy in efficient and environmentally sustainable ways. In the process of accessing and using energy, human societies have ripped up and flooded vast tracts of land and polluted air, water, and soil. The supply of some energy sources, such as oil, is limited, while other sources are simply too dirty to be sustainable. Finding sustainable sources of energy must become a priority for people around the world.

major sources of energy and related environmental issues

Fossil fuels (coal, oil, and natural gas)

· constituted approximately 85 percent of world commercial energy in 1997 (commercial energy refers to energy that is sold)

· environmental issues: supply, pollution from transportation spills, greenhouse gas emissions, and acid rain.

Hydroelectricity

· constituted approximately 7 percent of world commercial energy in 1997

· environmental issues: flooding of animal habitat and human settlements, mercury poisoning, and greenhouse gas emissions from decaying vegetation.

Nuclear

· constituted approximately 7 percent of world commercial energy in 1997

· environmental issues: storage of long-lasting radioactive waste and potential for major meltdown.

Alternatives (geothermal, solar, wind power)

· constituted less than 1 percent of world commercial energy in 1997

· these alternatives are renewable and have a lower impact on the environment, but there are political and economic obstacles preventing their widespread use. There are some other drawbacks to alternative energy sources, including noise pollution from wind farms, low efficiency in converting solar energy to usable forms, and the emission of hydrogen sulfide by geothermal reservoirs.

(Statistics from Peter H. Raven and Linda R. Berg, Environment *[Orlando, Fla.: Harcourt College Publishers, 2001].)*

faith connection

In the same way that the energy of the sun runs through all the systems of the physical world, so too does the spirit of the Creator flow through all of creation. While the natural world itself is not divine, the trace of the Creator's hand is evident in every leaf, in every storm, in every grain of sand. By virtue of this, the natural world connects people to God in a way which goes beyond words and understanding, but touches us at the very core of our beings. We find in creation a reminder of who made us who we are and gave us all we have, and to whom we owe our worship and praise.

FOR DISCUSSION AND REFLECTION

How has creation shaped your understanding of God?

for meditation

"For many of us, our first awareness of God and earliest intimations of peace are stirred by the beauty and harmony of creation. In the quiet of night and the breaking of day, in the bedrock of the mountains and the pulsing of the sea, in all that lives on the earth, we feel God living and moving. Behind and within creation we glimpse the hand of a creator—an animating spirit, a unifying presence, an underlying peace—so much greater than we."—Barbara A. Gerlach

for action

vacuum
fridge and freezer
condenser coils at
least once a year.

fill empty spaces
in freezer with gallons
of ice water.

use a slow cooker instead
of the oven.

clean
door gaskets
on the fridge and
freezer.

build a solar oven
and share a
"solar" meal with
friends.

decide what you want before
opening the fridge
or freezer.

find out
what energy sources
power electricity and heating
in your house, dormitory, or
apartment building. Are
there more sustainable
options available in your
area?

**use
a microwave
or toaster oven**
instead of the stove to
heat/cook small
portions of
food.

**turn
off
appliances**
(TV, computer, radio,
etc.) when not
in use.

**write your
electric or gas
company** communicating
your desire to have access
to heating and electricity
from sustainable
energy sources.

dust
light bulbs.

replace
incandescent
bulbs with compact
fluorescent light if a light
is used for more than
two hours a day.

**turn
off the lights**
when not in the room
(but leave lights on if
returning within fifteen
minutes—starting lights again
uses as much energy as
leaving them on).

WEEK 2
earth connection

At the top of the world lies an arctic paradise. Polar bears, arctic foxes, peregrine falcons, musk-oxen, Dall sheep, wolverines, snow geese, and caribou live here, as do mosses, lichens, and dwarf shrubs. It is also home to Aboriginal groups, many of whom still follow their traditional ways of life, including hunting caribou. This is Alaska's Arctic National Wildlife Refuge (ANWR).

ANWR has other treasures too: precious oil reserves lie beneath the frozen ground. And the U.S. government and energy industry believe ANWR could be the answer to their urgent desire to find more domestic sources of energy.

But at what cost? The tundra is a delicate environment due to its harsh climate, and oil development in the region could have a severe impact on the animals and plants, particularly the caribou. ANWR is a primary breeding ground for caribou herds which are the main food source for Aboriginal groups in both Alaska and the Yukon.

The debate raging between government, industry, and environmental groups is raising question over the comparative value of preserving wilderness over producing energy. Canadians and Americans enjoy luxuries and conveniences that require high energy consumption, but are they worth the sacrifice of a place like ANWR?

Fossil fuels
Fossil fuels include coal, petroleum (crude oil), and natural gas. These were formed from living organisms that decayed slowly over hundreds of millions of

years under extreme heat and pressure. Because they take so long to form, our supply is limited. Fossil fuels are nonrenewable resources. At current consumption rates, it is estimated that the Earth has enough coal to last for about a thousand years, but many experts expect that petroleum reserves will be used up during this century.

Fossil fuels have played an important role in advancing human technology, and they supply most of the energy used in industrialized societies. Their impact on the environment, however, can be devastating. The mining, transportation, and combustion of fossil fuels all create pollution.

- Coal mining releases acid, toxic minerals, and sediment into the soil and water.
- Oil spills, which can occur in the process of transportation, are destructive to habitat, and animal and plant life.
- Burning fossil fuels creates various pollutants, most notably carbon dioxide (a greenhouse gas), sulfur and nitrogen (which form into acid rain), and mercury. Coal is the dirtiest fossil fuel, petroleum is slightly cleaner, and natural gas is the cleanest.

FOR DISCUSSION AND REFLECTION

Do you think ANWR should be developed for oil extraction? Would you sacrifice driving your car one day per week to protect this fragile environment? Would you be willing to pay higher gas taxes to fund the development of more sustainable alternative fuel sources?

faith connection

After they were saved from slavery in Egypt, the people of Israel wandered in the desert for forty years. It was during this time in the wilderness that they were given the Law and were shaped into God's people. Moses encountered God in a burning bush at the far side of the desert and God spoke to Elijah on the mountain of God, after forty days and forty nights in the wilderness. Jesus began his ministry after being tested in the desert, and he often retreated to the mountains to pray.

The Bible is sprinkled with examples of God's people experiencing intense encounters with God in the wilderness, separated from human company and surrounded by the natural world. There is something about wild nature which facilitates intimate interactions with God. This was understood by early Christian hermits in the deserts of Egypt and by monks in remote monasteries. And today Christians build camps and retreat centres in forests and beside lakes, where they go to encounter God.

FOR DISCUSSION AND REFLECTION

What is your favourite retreat or place to encounter God?

for meditation
sanctuary

As I sink into my mossy seat,
The sounds of humans subside.
The peace of oblivion fills me
But I am not alone.

The coarse irregularity of the bark
Presses a pattern into my back.
The cool, wet air replenishes my lungs,
And surrounds my heart with vitality and life.

The little brook, which seeps from the hillside,
Sings gaily at my side
While timid wild flowers push
Their sincere faces through the grass.

This mossy chapel is my cathedral.
In this place, I meet my God.

This chapel has no roof, no walls,
Save majestic trees, the marble arches.
The golden altar is a simple wooden stand,
The richly carved pews are rotting logs.

But here, the song of the brook
Moves me more
Than the most glorious organ
And angel choirs from heaven
Could not sing as sweetly
As the birds above my head.

—Joanne Moyer

for action

have bicycle racks installed at your church, school, and workplace to encourage cyclists.

use energy-saving settings on refrigerators, dishwashers, washing machines, and clothes dryers.

carpool or use public transit for longer distances.

drive at moderate speeds (eg. 90km/h or 55 miles/h on the highway) to save energy and reduce pollution.

Choose a **fuel-efficient** vehicle.

walk or bike short distances.

have an energy audit done on your home, apartment, or dorm building.

Choose a home **close to work or school.**

When buying major appliances, **choose energy-efficient models**.

choose renewable energy sources for heating and electricity where available.

WEEK 3
earth connection

The Three Gorges Dam on the Yangtze river in China is the largest hydro-electric dam in the world. It has 29 turbines and will create a 600-kilometre reservoir. Once it is completed in 2009 this dam promises to generate 18,200 megawatts of power, offering a cleaner alternative than the coal which currently provides three-quarters of China's energy. The Chinese government is hailing the Three Gorges Project as a miracle. In addition to its energy production capacity, the dam should help control chronic flooding which endangers thousands of people, while its lock system should improve transportation to China's interior.

Beyond the hype, however, this feat of engineering is not quite so perfect. Over a million people will have to be resettled as their homes and farms become flooded. Refuse from flooded settlements, particularly hospitals and industrial sites, will pollute the river, while the slowing of the river's flow will cause accumulations of silt. Changes to the ecosystem, including increases in humidity and temperature, may negatively impact the river's flora and fauna, including already endangered species such as the Yangtze dolphin, the Chinese sturgeon, the Chinese tiger, the Chinese alligator, the Siberian crane, and the giant panda.

A series of smaller dams, which would not have the same high profile appeal, would be much less harmful to the social and ecological fabric and would possibly produce energy much more efficiently.

Countries like China, which are struggling to develop economically and meet the needs of massive populations, have an urgent need for supplies of energy. As the

Three Gorges Dam project illustrates, however, finding sustainable sources is a complicated and difficult task.

FOR DISCUSSION AND REFLECTION

One of the controversial issues surrounding the Kyoto Protocol is a concession allowing developing countries like China to have more time to meet energy emissions targets. Should developing countries be allowed to use cheaper, less sustainable energy sources to help them catch up economically? Should developing countries have to help pay for the pollution created by industrialized countries?

faith connection

"The heavens are telling the glory of God."—Psalm 19:1

Not only does creation reveal God and provide a place for encounter with God, but it praises God. The earth makes a joyful noise (Ps. 66:1) and sings a new song to the Lord (Ps. 96:1), trees clap their hands (Isa. 55:12), the sea roars, fields exult (Ps. 96:11-12) and hills sing together for joy (Ps. 98:8). Can you hear creation's praise in the song of the bird, in the roaring of the storm, in the waves lapping on the shore?

for meditation
psalm 148

Praise the Lord!
Praise the Lord from the heavens;
praise him from the heights!

Praise him, sun and moon;
praise him, all you shining stars!
Praise him, you highest heavens,
and you waters above the heavens!

Praise the Lord from the earth,
you sea monsters and all deeps,
fire and hail, snow and frost,
stormy winds fulfilling his command!

for action

use manual instead of electric appliances as much as possible.

run full loads in the washing machine and dishwasher.

clean lint from the dryer after use.

sort laundry for drying according to thickness of materials to avoid overdrying items, or remove clothing as it dries.

air-dry dishes in the dishwasher by using the efficiency cycle or by stopping the machine after the final rinse and opening the door.

hang dry laundry on clothesline or drying rack (this can be done outside and inside. Use a fan to facilitate drying inside).

Wash regular laundry in **cold water.**

Turn the **temperature setting** on your water heater to 43-49°C (110-120°F).

Make sure your **water heater** has an insulating blanket.

WEEK 4
earth connection welcome to the sustainable-energy city!

Feature attractions:

- solar panels, windmills, and small dams that produce clean, renewable energy
- crop waste, wood chips, and animal wastes that are converted to cooking fuel and burned to generate electricity
- fast and efficient public transit
- separate pathways for pedestrians and cyclists
- hybrid vehicles that produce little exhaust
- well-insulated houses and office buildings that don't need large furnaces; the heat generated by inhabitants' bodies, light bulbs, stoves, and other appliances provides sufficient heating
- strategically-placed trees and shrubs that help keep buildings cool.

As our sustainable-energy city shows, there are many different solutions to our global energy dilemma:

- there are alternative energy sources, which are both renewable and cleaner although there are some technical, economic, and political obstacles to developing many of them
- there are techniques for making energy production and use more efficient
- and there is conservation, which remains an important component to the solution.

Above any other solution, cutting our society's energy demands will do the most to reduce our impact on the environment.

faith connection creation: the ultimate object lesson

When Jesus wanted to teach or answer a question, he often told stories, or parables. Most of these parables illustrated his point using simple, everyday things, and many of them related to animals, birds, fish, and plants. The lilies of the field, the mustard tree, and the yeast in bread all have something to teach us about the kingdom of heaven and the way members of that kingdom should live.

"He said therefore, 'What is the kingdom of God like? And to what should I compare it? It is like a mustard seed that someone took and sowed in the garden; it grew and became a tree, and the birds of the air made nests in its branches.'"—Luke 13:18-19

FOR DISCUSSION AND REFLECTION

Day 1 has explored the ways in which creation is a revelation of God. How does this affect the way you value creation and the way you treat creation?

for meditation
nature's creed

I believe in the brook as it wanders
*   From hillside into glade;*
I believe in the breeze as it whispers
*   When evening's shadows fade.*
I believe in the roar of the river
*   As it dashes from high cascade;*
I believe in the cry of the tempest
*   Mid the thunder's cannonade.*
I believe in the light of shining stars,
*   I believe in the sun and moon*

I believe in the flash of lightning,
*   I believe in the night-bird's croon*
I believe in the faith of the flowers,
*   I believe in the rock and sod,*
For in all of these appeareth clear
*   The handiwork of God.*

— Author Unknown

for action

close registers and doors to unused rooms.

change furnace filters twice a year.

plant shade trees and shrubs around house to help cooling (deciduous trees on south and west side of house).

clean or replace furnace, air-conditioner, and heat pump filters.

close blinds and curtains during the day to block sun.

in hot weather, set the thermostat at 78° F or higher, use ceiling and floor fans.

keep fireplace dampers closed when not in use.

take a field trip to a wind farm or an energy-sustainable building.

in cold weather, set the thermostat at 68° F or lower and dress warmly. Lower the thermostat at night, in unoccupied rooms, and when you are not home.

do not block heating vents or air grills with drapes or large furniture.

rope caulk leaky windows to seal up air leaks.

place fillers in electrical outlets to stop drafts from exterior walls.

install solar panels on your roof to supplement your energy supply.

an echo of all creation

Yesterday the rains stopped and I went to work in our wood lot. The scrubbed air was sparkling like champagne with a vital effervescence. On every pendulous fir needle was a diamond drop of water catching and reflecting a prism of sunlight. When I peered closely at a drop, it mirrored the forest around and behind me in a convex bubble. This bespoke to me that each and every bit of God's handiwork is an echo of all creation.—*7-Days trek participant*

the blue planet . . .

Day 2 : **the blue planet**

"Our liquid planet glows like a soft blue sapphire in the hard-edged darkness of space. There is nothing else like it in the solar system."—John Todd

air and water are the two most defining characteristics of our planet. They are also two of the most basic necessities of life. Day 2 examines issues relating to the quality and quantity of air and water. Day 2 also explores God's role as Lord of creation and begins to look at the role humans play in creation.

"And God said, 'Let there be a dome in the midst of the waters, and let it separate the waters from the waters.' So God made the dome and separated the waters that were under the dome from the waters that were above the dome. And it was so. God called the dome Sky. And there was evening and there was morning, the second day."

—Genesis 1:6-8

WEEK 1
earth connection

Mexico City is the most polluted city in the world; breathing its air is like smoking two packs of cigarettes a day. Pollutants are spewed from old cars burning fuel laced with contaminants and are trapped over the city by surrounding mountains. Despite a decade of efforts to improve the city's air quality by replacing old vehicles, switching to unleaded gasoline, instituting driving restrictions, and reforesting nearby hillsides, the city was still experiencing pollution emergencies as recently as 1999.

Cities worldwide are suffering from deteriorating air quality, caused mainly by industry and transportation. Photochemical smog (which forms from vehicle emissions) reduces visibility, poses health risks to humans and animals, and stresses plant growth. Acid rain (a consequence of industrial processes) destroys lakes, forests, and buildings. While countries in the global North have more cars and more factories, they also have better air quality standards and more resources to invest in prevention and remediation. In developing countries, like Mexico, environmental standards are deliberately lowered to attract investors, vehicles and equipment are older and usually pollute more, and there is a lack of resources to invest in pollution control. For these reasons, air pollution tends to be worse in the large cities of the global South.

Improving air quality must begin by preventing the initial release of pollutants into the atmosphere rather than focussing on cleaning them up after they are there.

It is often said that people in the global North export their environmental problems to countries in the global South (like Mexico). Do you agree? What can we do to rectify this situation?

faith connection

Human beings often like to think that the Earth was made for us and that it is ours to do with as we please. After all, we were made only a little lower than angels and given dominion over all other creatures (Ps. 8:5-8). This attitude is called anthropocentrism: the belief that humans are at the centre of everything. While human beings have been given special abilities and privileges, the anthropocentric position is egotistical, and it ignores a very important truth—that God is the true owner and ruler of creation. Psalm 24:1-2 proclaims: "The earth is the Lord's and all that is in it, the world, and those who live in it; for he has founded it on the seas, and established it on the rivers." Remembering our creaturehood and the sovereignty of our Creator is necessary to building a peaceful relationship with the Earth.

FOR DISCUSSION AND REFLECTION
What are examples of anthropocentric attitudes and actions in our society and daily lives?

for meditation

All gifts of nature and of grace
have been given us on loan. Their ownership is not ours,
but God's.
God never gave personal
property to anyone—
not . . . to any other person
or to any creature in any way.
Treat all things as if they were loaned to you
without any ownership—
whether body or soul,
sense or strength,
external goods or honors,
friends or relations,
house or hall,
everything.
For if I want to possess
the property I have
instead of receive it on loan
then I want to be a master.

—Meister Eckhart

for action

avoid using aerosol cans
and styrofoam containing CFCs.

Use **ethanol-blended** fuel.

walk or cycle
instead of driving—it's good for the air and good for your health.

when buying a new vehicle,
choose a fuel-efficient model.

write a letter
to your elected representative asking for stricter air quality standards.

Have your **vehicle tuned** regularly.

avoid idling
your car.

take public transit
or carpool.

If you are moving, try to **find a home close to work** and school.

plant trees
in your community.

WEEK 2
earth connection is your house sick?

Air in enclosed spaces such as buildings often has much higher levels of pollutants than are found outside. This is a sobering fact considering that most Canadians and Americans spend 90-95 percent of their time indoors. Indoor pollutants may infiltrate a building from outside sources, as is the case with radon, a naturally occurring gas which can seep into homes and cause lung cancer. They may also originate from chemicals that are used or produced inside the building, such as cigarette smoke and formaldehyde, which is emitted by things like building materials, furniture, upholstery, insulation, and fingernail hardener. Other sources of indoor air pollution include office machinery, cleaning materials, and air fresheners.

More and more people are suffering from eye irritation, nausea, headaches, respiratory infections, depression, and fatigue because their indoor environments are polluted. These problems have increased dramatically in recent decades as newer buildings contain more and more synthetic materials and have decreased quality of ventilation. At the same time, biological agents such as dust, mould, and fungi can be problematic in older houses. Bad indoor air quality prevents students from working and is a rising cause of worker absenteeism. More and more businesses, schools, and individuals are reconsidering what they use to build, furnish, and maintain their buildings.

FOR DISCUSSION AND REFLECTION
What do you do to make your home or workplace a healthy environment?

faith connection

The Creator's sovereignty over the Earth is manifest in many ways and serves as a humble reminder to humans who tend toward selfish arrogance. God is the Lord of sea, wind, and storm and has control over all the Earth's processes (Job 38, Ps. 29). Furthermore, all the products of the Earth are gifts from God's hand. It is through God's grace, and not the effort of humans, that the Earth is alive and fruitful. God gave the Israelites manna in the wilderness and led them to a land of milk and honey, and God continues to bless the creatures of the Earth with sun, rain, and food.

for meditation

You visit the earth and water it,
  you greatly enrich it;
the river of God is full of water;
  you provide the people with grain,
for so you have prepared it.
You water its furrows abundantly,
  settling its ridges,
softening it with showers,
  and blessing its growth.
You crown the year with your bounty;
  your wagon tracks overflow with richness.
The pastures of the wilderness overflow,
  the hills gird themselves with joy,
the meadows clothe themselves with flocks,
  the valleys deck themselves with grain,
they shout and sing together for joy.

—Psalm 65:9-13

You make springs gush forth in the valleys;
  they flow between the hills,
giving drink to every wild animal;
  the wild asses quench their thirst.
By the streams the birds of the air have their habitation;
  they sing among the branches.
From your lofty abode you water the mountains;
  the earth is satisfied with the fruit of your work.

—Psalm 104:10-13

for action

remove your shoes before entering your house or apartment to reduce inputs of dust, lead, and pesticides.

Replace carpeting with **wood or linoleum.**

ensure that woodburning stoves and fire-places are properly ventilated.

avoid use of aerosol spray products and commercial room deodorizers or air fresheners—boil cloves or cin-namon on your stove or in a potpourri holder instead.

ventilate your house or apartment by opening windows regularly or by installing air-to-air heat exchangers.

Avoid buying furniture and other products containing **formaldehyde.**

grow house plants—spider plants, aloe vera, and elephant ear philodendron are some plants that are especially effective at removing toxins from the air.

test your home for radon, formaldehyde, and asbestos fibres.

when doing renovations, use paint and building mate-rials that release the least amount of fumes and chemicals.

WEEK 3
earth connection

In the deserts of Kazakstan and Uzbekistan, rusted fishing boats sit surrounded by miles of sand. The Aral Sea, in which these boats once sailed, used to be the world's fourth-largest freshwater lake; now it is the eighth largest. Its demise is due primarily to the diversion of water for irrigation, and the consequences have been devastating.

The Sea itself has lost 80 percent of its volume and the former lake bed is a broad salt pan desert. Without the climate-moderating functions of the sea, the local climate is more continental, and the growing season has shortened. Dust storms spread salt and pesticide residue over a large area. Health conditions for nearby residents have also deteriorated, with increases in the incidence of cancer, kidney disease, cholera, respiratory problems, and birth defects. Nearly all the aquatic life in the lake has disappeared as salt levels have risen, and the fishing industry has collapsed. Ironically, agricultural productivity has also decreased.

Attempts to save or at least slow the deterioration of the Aral Sea area have repeatedly faltered due to political complications and the desire for short-term economic gain. Even if water diversion stopped today, the chances of restoring the lake to its former size and vitality are slim.

Water is one of the most basic necessities of life, and it seems to be in infinite supply. It flows through rivers, collects in lakes and oceans, and falls from the sky. Three quarters of the Earth's surface is covered with water, but only a small percentage is usable for most purposes:

- 97 percent of the Earth's water is salty
- 1.984 percent of the Earth's water is caught in glaciers, ice sheets, and underground aquifers
- just over 0.01 percent of the Earth's water is fresh and accessible for use.

Freshwater shortages are caused by climate, drought, deforestation, overgrazing, and human uses, which include irrigation, industrial processes, the generation of electricity and household use.
- Canadians use 1500 cubic metres of water annually
- one person in the global North uses 350-1000 litres of water daily
- one person in the global South uses 2-5 litres of water daily.

Water is becoming more and more scarce in many parts of the world and factors such as climate change, deforestation, and human population growth are making the situation worse. Some experts predict that water will be as precious in the twenty-first century as oil was in the twentieth century. Improving efficiency of water use, conserving water and preventing water pollution are needed to protect and ensure a water supply for future generations.

(Statistics from Erin Crisfield, God's People, God's Planet: Living lightly on the earth [Toronto, Ont.: The Presbyterian Church of Canada, 2001], 20; G. Tyler Miller, Sustaining the Earth. 5th ed. [Belmont, Calif.: Brooks/Cole Thomson Learning, 2002], 293-294.)

FOR DISCUSSION AND REFLECTION
Canada has 15 to 20 percent of the world's freshwater by volume, while many regions in the U.S., especially in the southwest, are facing increasing water shortages. This will likely become a source of conflict in the future. How should

these two nations resolve their water differences? Should Canada allow bulk exportation of its water? Should the U.S. allow itself to become as dependent on other nations for water as it is for oil? How would a Christian perspective inform this debate?

faith connection

Rejection of our creaturehood and the refusal to submit to the will of the Creator is one of the greatest temptations of human beings. Such acts of sinfulness and rebellion have an impact on the rest of creation. When Adam and Eve ate the forbidden fruit, they were banished from the garden and the ground was cursed (Gen. 3). From the very beginning of time, the moral choices of people have had an effect on the state of creation and on our relationship with it.

When human beings choose to rebel against God—to live in greed rather than generosity and in willfulness rather than obedience—the relationships among people, and between people and the land, are disrupted. Sometimes this occurs as a direct result of human action; for instance, if the Israelites did not abide by the agricultural practices laid out in the Sabbath laws, the land would be depleted and would no longer produce food. At other times God deliberately used the forces of nature to punish human sinfulness: "He turns rivers into a desert, springs of water into thirsty ground, a fruitful land into a salty waste, because of the wickedness of its inhabitants" (Ps. 107:33-34). And sometimes it is the response of the land itself: "Hear the word of the LORD, O people of Israel; for the LORD has an indictment against the inhabitants of the land. There is no faithfulness or loyalty, and no knowledge of God in the land. Swearing, lying, and murder, and stealing and adultery break out; bloodshed follows bloodshed. Therefore the land mourns, and all who live in it languish; together with the wild animals and the birds of the air, even the fish of the sea are perishing" (Hos. 4:1-3).

FOR DISCUSSION AND REFLECTION

The Old Testament makes a clear link between human sinfulness and the state of the Earth. What do you think about this connection? Is human sinfulness related to the current environmental crisis? In what way?

for meditation

God desires that all the world
be pure in God's sight.

The earth should not be injured.
The earth should not
be destroyed.

As often as the elements,
the elements of the world,
are violated by ill-treatment,
so God will cleanse them.

God will cleanse them
through sufferings,
through hardships
of humankind.

The high, the low,
all of creation,
God gives to humankind to use.

If this privilege is misused,
God's justice permits creation
to punish humanity.

—Hildegard of Bingen

for action

Avoid using the toilet as a **garbage can.**

turn off the tap when brushing teeth, shaving, or washing.

Keep a jug of **drinking water** in the fridge.

flush the toilet only when necessary. ("If it's yellow, let it mellow; if it's brown, flush it down.").

check for and fix toilet bowl and faucet leaks. (Check for leaks in your toilet by putting food colouring in the tank. If after 15 minutes the colour shows up in the toilet bowl, there is a leak.)

take short showers instead of baths—turn off the water while soaping and shampooing; then quickly rinse off.

find out where your water comes from and learn about your watershed (the land area that feeds the water source).

when washing dishes by hand, do not let the tap run continuously.

install low-flow faucet aerators on sink and shower taps.

only run the dishwasher with a full load—wash small or medium loads of dishes by hand.

install a low-flush toilet or use a water displacement device (like a plastic jug filled with water) in your toilet tank to reduce amount of water used to flush.

Rinse vegetables in a **stoppered sink.**

choose a front-loader washing machine (requires less water than top-loading machines).

Install a **composting toilet.**

thaw food in the fridge instead of under running water.

do not use a garbage disposal system—consider composting instead.

wash only full loads in the washing machine and use the shortest cycle possible.

wash the car on the lawn— the lawn gets watered at the same time.

recycle grey water in your home. (Grey water is water that has been in sinks, showers, washing machines, and dishwashers. It can b used for flushing toilets, washing th car, or watering the lawn. This requires some modifications to your plumbing system.)

insulate hot water pipes to keep heat in (it won't be necessary to run the tap for as long to get hot water).

clean the car with a bucket of water and sponge, not the garden hose.

Clean sidewalks and driveways **with a broom instead of a hose.**

Use a soaker hose or apply water slowly **to the base of plants** rather than the leaves.

Water the lawn or garden **during the cool part of the day** to reduce evaporation.

collect water in a rainbarrel to use for watering plants.

Landscape your yard with vegetation that requires **little or no irrigation.**

Use lawn fertilizers **sparingly.**

conserve moisture in your lawn by cutting the grass to a height of 5 to 8 cm and leaving the clippings on the ground—this keeps the roots shaded and moist.

Keep soil fertile and moist by **using mulches** around plants and trees, and compost in the garden.

use drip irrigation—large amounts of water are lost by sprinklers which spray water into the air.

WEEK 4
earth connection

Twenty-five years ago, swimming in the Hamilton Harbour on Lake Ontario would have been unthinkable. Over a period of about 250 years, the harbour was used as a garbage can for the city, its industry and the surrounding agricultural communities. Pollutants that were poured into the harbour and its watershed included fertilizers, pesticides, herbicides, and industrial and human waste, which contain metallic, organic, and bacterial contaminants. As a result, fish and wildlife populations declined, while human health problems increased.

Recently, however, the Hamilton Harbour has experienced a remarkable renewal. During the late 1980s, the Hamilton Harbour was identified as one of 43 Areas of Concern in the Great Lakes area and in 1992, a Remedial Action Plan (RAP) was developed to address the environmental concerns in the harbour. One of the reasons for the RAP's success is the fact that it was developed with the cooperation of all three levels of government, industrial and commercial interests, environmental groups, and members of the public. The combined knowledge and input of these diverse stakeholders enabled those working on the harbour cleanup to have a balanced and comprehensive approach and today people can safely swim in Hamilton Harbour for the first time in decades.

a primer on water pollution

The hydrologic cycle, which is the natural process by which water is transferred from the atmosphere to the earth's surface and back again, has features that purify water very effectively. The passage of water through wetlands, in particular, is instrumental in the purification process. If, however, water is overloaded with materials which break down slowly or are completely nondegradable, the system becomes overloaded and pollution builds up. This is happening to water systems all over the world.

types of pollution
· oxygen-demanding waste which degrades the environment for fish and aquatic plants
· infectious agents, such as bacteria and viruses, which usually come from animal or human waste
· nutrients from fertilizers which cause excessive growth of algae
· organic chemicals such as pesticides
· inorganic chemicals such as acids and metals from mining and industrial processes
· sediment from land erosion which prevents sunlight from penetrating into the water
· radioactive substances, mostly from mining
· heat from industry.

Steps necessary to improve water quality include improving wastewater treatment, reducing the use of polluting products, improving industrial processes, strengthening environmental legislation and restoring wetlands.

FOR DISCUSSION AND REFLECTION
Are there environmentally degraded areas near you which have been restored? Are there areas you would like to see restored?

faith connection

"So God created humankind in his image . . . God blessed them, and God said to them, 'Be fruitful and multiply, and fill the earth and subdue it; and have dominion over the fish of the sea and over the birds of the air and over every living thing that moves upon the earth.'"—Genesis 1:27-28

Human beings are not the owners or rulers of the earth. Rather, we are called into relationship with both the Creator and the other creatures. This relationship is fundamentally covenantal: God cares for all of creation, and therefore expects a certain response from it. God relates to creation through faithfulness, patience and graciousness rather than coercion, granting creatures a great deal of freedom and autonomy. At the same time, creation is not left entirely to its own devices: there are restraints and limitations placed on its freedom. This might be described as disciplined liberty. As humans, our covenantal task in response to God's care is to discover the extent of our liberty and the necessary bounds of our discipline.

FOR DISCUSSION AND REFLECTION

Does Psalm 8 present the same understandings of the place of human beings in creation as the reflection in this Faith Connection? Do you agree with the presentation of human beings in Psalm 8?

for meditation

O Lord our Sovereign,
  how majestic is your name in all the earth!

When I look at your heavens, the work of your fingers,
  the moon and the stars that you have established;
what are human beings that you are mindful of them,
  mortals that you care for them?

Yet you have made them a little lower than God,
  and crowned them with glory and honor.
You have given them dominion over the works of your hands;
  you have put all things under their feet,
all sheep and oxen,
  and also the beasts of the field,
the birds of the air, and the fish of the sea,
  whatever passes along the paths of the seas.
O Lord, our Sovereign,
  how majestic is your name in all the earth!

—Psalm 8:1, 3-9

for action

use completely (or share with other people) all contents of strong chemical cleaners, paints, polishes, and glues—donate leftover paint to theatre groups or shelters.

use phosphate-free and biodegradable laundry detergent and cleaners.

Do not use **water fresheners** in the toilet.

use latex (water-based) instead of oil-based paint whenever possible.

avoid pouring hazardous products down the drain or flushing them down the toilet. Take them to local recycling or disposal facilities. (Common household hazardous products include: antifreeze, nail polish remover, toilet cleaners, chlorine bleach, drain cleaners, paints, pesticides, pool chemicals, used motor oil, and prescription drugs.)

use manure, compost, or grass clippings instead of inorganic fertilizers in garden and on lawn.

learn more about environmentally friendly household products at www.environmental-choice.com.

alternative cleaning compounds:

pure soap

Good all-purpose cleaner, mix 30 ml (2 Tbsp) of flakes with 1 L (4 cups) of water for indoor plant, shrub, and tree insecticide

baking soda

Good for scouring and deodorizing

recipe for all-purpose cleaner

- 3.8 L (1 gallon) hot water
- 60 ml (1/4 cup) borax
- 60 ml (1/4 cup) vinegar
- 30 ml (2 Tbsp) liquid soap
- 60 ml (1/4 cup) ammonia (optional)
- elbow grease

vinegar

Mix with equal parts water for glass cleaner, use undiluted to remove mildew

natural oils

Use 5 ml (1 tsp) lemon oil with 1/2 litre (2 cups) mineral oil or olive oil to polish furniture

washing soda

Dissolve 3 ml (1/2 tsp) in hot water for a drain cleaner or mix with equal parts ammonia for an all-purpose cleaner

borax

Good for deodorizing and cleaning floors, walls, and tiles—natural mould inhibitor

the uncontained God

I stood on a beach in the middle of a typhoon. The wind caused the sand to pelt against me and the trees to sway back and forth. The rain had drenched me within a few seconds. The ocean wave pounded the shore causing the water to run between the houses. All of this screamed of a God who is not contained. He is not contained in our churches or our theories. He is wild, majestic, and powerful.—*7-Days trek participant*

the holy earth . . .

Day 3 : **the holy earth**

The Eleventh Commandment:

"Thou shalt inherit the holy earth as a faithful steward, conserving its resources and productivity from generation to generation. Thou shalt safeguard thy fields from soil erosion, thy living waters from drying up, thy forests from desolation and protect thy hills from overgrazing by thy herds, that thy descendants may have abundance forever. If any shall fail in this stewardship of the land thy fruitful fields shall become sterile stony ground and wasting gullies, and thy descendants shall decrease and live in poverty or perish from the face of the earth."—Dr. C. W. Lowdermilk

day 3 addresses land stewardship, from both a faith and an ecological perspective. The faith perspective explores the special role that humanity has to play in creation. The ecological perspective looks at what we take out and what we put into the Earth, and how these activities impact its resources and productivity.

"And God said, 'Let the waters under the sky be gathered together into one place, and let the dry land appear.' And it was so. God called the dry land Earth, and the waters that were gathered together he called Seas. And God saw that it was good. Then God said, 'Let the earth put forth vegetation: plants yielding seed, and fruit trees of every kind bearing fruit with the seed in it.' And it was so. The earth brought forth vegetation: plants yielding seed, and fruit trees of every kind bearing fruit with the seed in it. And God saw that it was good. And there was evening and there was morning, the third day."—Genesis 1:9-13

WEEK 1
earth connection

In northern Somalia, grandmothers can remember when lions could be heard roaring in the surrounding grasslands. Today the grass and the lions are gone, along with the trees and other wildlife. A long-running civil war has forced city people to flee to isolated areas, and they do not understand the delicate balance necessary to survive in these fragile, drought-prone environments. With no other source of income, they have resorted to cutting trees to make charcoal to sell. The results are soil erosion, drought, and increasing desertification. Some of the grandmothers, who remember the lions and the acacia trees that once were, are working to bring them back.

soil degradation and desertification

Degradation of soils is a problem around the world. Major issues include soil erosion, the depletion of nutrients, and desertification. Desertification occurs when existing deserts expand or new deserts form on land that was once productive. This is especially an issue in arid countries, like China and much of Africa. The United Nations Convention to Combat Desertification estimates that 100 million hectares (247 million acres) of fertile land are lost every year, threatening food security for 1.2 billion people.

causes of desertification

- overcultivation
- overgrazing
- deforestation
- poor irrigation practices.

consequences of desertification

- reduced resilience of land to natural variations in climate
- reduced soil productivity
- damaged vegetation
- dust storms
- flooding and drought
- threat to food security
- displacement of human populations, which can lead to conflict.

FOR DISCUSSION AND REFLECTION

War is a root cause of desertification in Somalia. What are other examples of human conflict are causing threat to the natural environment?

faith connection

"So God created humankind in his image, in the image of God he created them, male and female he created them."—Genesis 1:27

Humankind was created in the image of God, and this distinguishes us from the rest of creation. But what does this distinction mean? This is a difficult question to answer, but it seems that the relationship between God and creation is somehow manifested most intensely in human beings. God has made an especially close commitment to us and we are given greater freedom in responding. We have also been delegated with special responsibilities: we are given dominion ". . . over the fish of the sea and over the birds of the air and over every living thing that moves upon the earth" (Gen. 1:28). The special gifts and status that are bestowed upon humans are given to enable us to fulfill the tasks which God has assigned to us. Human beings are creatures to whom much has been given, but of whom much is expected.

FOR DISCUSSION AND REFLECTION

What do you think being created in the image of God means? How does this relate us as humans to the natural world?

for meditation

We have forgotten who we are.

We have forgotten who we are.
We have alienated ourselves from the unfolding of the cosmos.
We have become estranged from the movements of the earth.
We have turned our backs on the cycles of life.

We have forgotten who we are.

We have sought only our own security.
We have exploited simply for our own ends.
We have distorted our knowledge.
We have abused our power.

We have forgotten who we are.

Now the land is barren and the waters are poisoned
And the air is polluted.

We have forgotten who we are.

Now the forests are dying and the creatures are disappearing
And humans are despairing.

We have forgotten who we are.

We ask forgiveness.
We ask for the gift of remembering.
We ask for the strength to change.

We have forgotten who we are.

— U.N. Environmental Sabbath

for action

reduce use of wood and paper products.

Put a **"no flyers"** sign on your mailbox.

share newspapers, magazines, and books with friends.

Use newspaper or cloth bags to **wrap gifts**.

make envelopes out of old magazines.

Purchase **recycled** paper products.

use both sides of every sheet of paper—if you don't already have one, set aside a box or file for paper used on one side to be reused in your computer printer or as scrap paper.

WEEK 2
earth connection

Kenora, Ontario, is an idyllic sort of place. Situated on the Canadian Shield, it is surrounded by lakes, forests, and vibrant wildlife, and residents and tourists alike enjoy camping, hiking, and fishing. But if you drive about an hour north, the scene becomes less peaceful. Instead of tall forests, there are wide open spaces covered in bits and pieces of trees left by clear-cutting, and the traffic consists mostly of logging trucks. Not on all the roads, however, because some of the logging roads are being blocked by members of the Grassy Narrows First Nation (with support from Christian Peacemaker Teams) in an attempt to save their traditional lands from the ravages of clear-cutting. The pulp and paper industry destroys the forest which houses animals and medicinal plants, and it poisons the water and ground with mercury, oil spills, garbage, pesticides, and abandoned cut trees. Not only does this activity interfere with the Aboriginal people's traditional right to hunt and gather, but it also damages the economy and quality of life in Kenora and other surrounding communities.

The boreal forest, which covers the northern sections of North America, Europe, and Russia, is the northern equivalent of the rainforest. It is a wildlife haven (housing moose, deer, martens, rabbits, beavers, foxes, wolves, bears, eagles, and various birds) and it contributes to water and air purification. It also provides human beings with many of our needs and luxuries.

deforestation

Deforestation is a serious problem in forests around the world. Reasons for deforestation include:

- clearing land for agriculture and cattle ranching
- harvesting wood for paper, furniture, lumber, and other wood products.

The consequences of deforestation include:
- loss of plant species
- loss of animal habitat (the biggest cause of species extinction)
- decreased soil fertility
- soil erosion
- increased flooding and droughts
- increased global temperatures due to the release of carbon stored in trees.

FOR DISCUSSION AND REFLECTION
Which of the forest's benefits do you most enjoy?

faith connection

Human beings have special responsibilities toward creation: according to Genesis 1, humans are to subdue creation and have dominion over it. This has been interpreted as a license to use and abuse it as we please. But is that what God really intends? Human responsibility in creation is often understood in terms of stewardship. A steward is a staff member who manages the affairs or property of his or her superior, acting as a representative of that superior. To be faithful stewards, we as human beings need to ask ourselves how God rules over creation, and we need to take our cues from God's example. We may also get some hints from the stories of kingship in ancient Israel. Israelite kings were, in a sense, stewards over God's people. Although few of them lived up to God's standards, Israel's kings were expected to lead the people in keeping their covenant with God and to protect their people's well-being through the promotion of justice through care for the poor and underprivileged. According to Scripture, an ideal king's rule should promote harmony, fertility, and prosperity in his kingdom (Deut. 17:14-20; Ps. 72). Does human rule over creation today promote these things?

FOR DISCUSSION AND REFLECTION

What does stewardship mean to you? What are examples of good stewardship that you have observed or experienced?

for meditation

Give the king your justice, O God,
   and your righteousness to a king's son.
May he judge your people with righteousness,
   and your poor with justice.
May the mountains yield prosperity for the people,
   and the hills, in righteousness.
May he defend the cause of the poor of the people,
   give deliverance to the needy,
   and crush the oppressor.

May he live while the sun endures,
   and as long as the moon, throughout all generations.
May he be like rain that falls on the mown grass,
   like showers that water the earth.
In his days may righteousness flourish
   and peace abound, until the moon is no more.

—Psalm 72:1-7

for action

Look for wood products that are certified for **sustainable forestry practices.** Two certification programs are: the Good-Wood seal given by the Friends of the Earth; and the Forest Stewardship Council, at www.fscoax.org/.

donate old magazines to waiting rooms, libraries, day care centres, schools, and civic organizations.

send back junk mail that comes with an envelope with pre-paid postage. Make sure your name and address doesn't appear but encourage the receiver to recycle the paper.

print church bulletins on both sides—have recycling bins handy at the back of the church.

plant trees on your church property and in your yard. Have a tree planting party.

avoid buying wood furniture made from teakwood, mahogany, or other woods harvested from the endangered rain forest.

Collect one-sided printed documents for **scrap paper**, or for Sunday school artwork.

WEEK 3

earth connection heaven and earth shall pass away, but not our plastics

"Mennonite workers in Somalia were traveling through the countryside one day near the southern seaport of Kismayo, when they came upon the remains of a cow. Its skin, hair, and flesh was gone. All that remained to mark its place of death was its skeleton and stomach. Inside the stomach, which had dried out and was now transparent, the Mennonites could see an oil filter, a piece of plastic window screen, and a blue plastic bag. Whether or not the cow died from ingesting these relics of our throw-away 'civilization' is not the only question. Another question is: Should our garbage outlive us?"
—Myron Sommers, former MCC worker in Somalia

Canadians and Americans produce the most waste per capita in the world. During the 1990s, Canadians threw away an average of one ton of garbage per person per year. According to data from the U.S. Environmental Protection Agency, Americans throw away:

- enough aluminum to rebuild the U.S.'s entire commercial airline fleet every three months
- enough tires each year to encircle the planet almost three times
- 19 million computers and 8 million TV sets every year
- 2.5 million plastic bottles every hour
- 670,000 metric tons of edible food per year.

what did you throw out today?

Solid wastes are problematic because they have to be put somewhere. This takes up space especially since materials like plastic decompose very slowly. But plastics aren't the only problem—even biodegradable substances, like food and paper, decompose slowly when they are compacted in landfills without much oxygen. Moisture filtering through landfills and dumps can pick up toxins and pollute ground water, while the decomposition process produces carbon dioxide and methane, which are greenhouse gases. Incineration is another option for waste disposal, but it creates air pollution and ashes which must still be disposed of in a landfill. And finally, North American throw-away society means a continuous demand for new products, causing a huge drain on natural resources.

(Statistics from G. Tyler Miller, Sustaining the Earth, *5th ed. [Belmont, Calif.: Brooks/Cole Thomson Learning, 2002], 331.)*

FOR DISCUSSION AND REFLECTION

List all the things you threw in the garbage today. What could have been reused, restored, recycled, or shared?

faith connection

Genesis 2 provides another model of humanity's role in creation. This model is more passive than the one in Genesis 1, but it also shows the harsh consequences of misusing our power and privilege. God places Adam in the garden "to till it and keep it." Adam is supposed to take care of the garden and the earth to preserve it, but his responsibilities do not involve a great deal of effort, nor does he need to alter or interfere with God's handiwork. God has provided for all of Adam and Eve's needs—the garden has already been planted and food is abundant—so really, all they have to do is observe and enjoy the bounty of the garden.

This idyllic arrangement, however, is destroyed the moment Adam and Eve defy the limits that have been placed on them by eating from the forbidden tree. They are banished from the garden, and the Earth no longer provides so generously for their needs. We are still suffering the consequences of this rift in the covenant with God, and in the relationship between humans and creation. The responsibility of caring for the cosmos is an enormous one, and the consequences of failure are equally monumental.

FOR DISCUSSION AND REFLECTION

Some people see a significant difference between the role of human beings in creation as portrayed in Genesis 1 and in Genesis 2. Do you think these models are complementary or contradictory?

for meditation

O God, how long will it take
before we awaken to what we have done?
How many waters must we pollute?
How many woodlots must we destroy?
How many forests must we despoil?
How much soil must we erode and poison, O God?
How much of the earth's atmosphere
must we contaminate?
How many species
must we abuse and extinguish?
How many people
must we degrade and kill with toxic wastes,
before we learn to love you
and respect your creation;
before we learn to love and respect our home?

For our wrongs,
we ask forgiveness.

In sorrow for what we have done
we offer repentance.
We pray that our actions
toward you and your creation
are worthy of our repentance;
that we will so act here on earth
that heaven will not be a shock to us.

May your realm come and
your will be done on earth! AMEN

—The North American Conference on
Christianity and Ecology

use refillable/reusable containers for lunches, leftovers, and beverages.

do a waste audit—during this week, monitor what you throw out.

for action

learn where your waste and sewage goes.

Use **cloth bags** for shopping.

Buy products made from **recycled materials.**

buy in bulk and avoid food packaged in individual servings.

practice the five rs: revere, reduce, repair, reuse, recycle.

use cloth napkins, handkerchiefs, diapers, and cleaning rags.

Use **rechargeable** batteries.

donate old clothes to charity— this week, go through your closet and set aside for donation clothing that you no longer wear.

refill ink cartridges from your computer printer.

provide recycling facilities at home, church, work, and school.

avoid disposable products as much as possible. Use reusable dishes and table clothes for church functions.

reuse egg cartons or donate them to schools, day cares, or community centres for crafts.

Educate your family and friends about **recycling**.

protest excess packaging by unwrapping over-packaged goods in the store or writing to manufacturers.

Plan a **garbage clean-up day** in your neighbourhood.

If your community does not have a **curbside pick-up program**, lobby your local government to start one.

WEEK 4
earth connection

"There was once a town in the heart of America where all life seemed to live in harmony with its surroundings . . . Then a strange blight crept over the area and everything began to change . . . Mysterious maladies swept the flocks of chickens; the cattle and sheep sickened and died. . .There was a strange stillness . . .The few birds seen anywhere were moribund; they trembled violently and could not fly. It was a spring without voices."
—Rachel Carson

So begins *Silent Spring*, a book published in 1962 by American zoologist Rachel Carson. She warned that a spring might come in which there would be no bird songs because they would have all been wiped out by the indiscriminate use of pesticides.

Pesticides have yielded many benefits since their discovery during World War II. They are an important element of conventional North American agriculture and have contributed significantly to increases in food production in many parts of the world. They also have helped to control diseases spread by insects, such as malaria, typhus, and the West Nile virus and they allow people to enjoy the outdoors without being eaten alive by bugs. When misused, however, their effects can be devastating. Of particular concern are chemicals which take a long time to break down and travel through the food web, collecting in greater and more dangerous concentrations in animals at the upper end of the food chain, such as birds of prey, large predators, and human beings.

Pesticides work by disrupting body processes, such as the nervous system, or the functioning of a major organ. In humans, short-term pesticide poisoning can cause symptoms such as nausea and headaches, and may result in permanent damage to the nervous system and even death. Long-term effects include cancer, sterility, and delayed development of intellectual and motor skills in children. Some pesticides, known as endocrine disrupters, behave like hormones and cause reproductive problems in animals and possibly humans. In addition to their dangerous effects, the overuse or misuse of pesticides is often counter-productive. When exposed to large amounts of pesticides, pests can develop resistance to the pesticide, reducing its effectiveness. At the same time, non-target insects and plants are often also killed. Some nontarget insects, such as dragonflies or ladybugs, actually help in getting rid of the target pests because they eat other insects.

Largely because of Rachel Carson's courageous work, pesticide use has become much more strictly regulated. Certain pesticides (such as DDT) have been banned in many countries, but are often still manufactured and sold to countries in the global South where regulations are less stringent. Lawn pesticides also pose a problem because they are not regulated as strictly as agricultural pesti-cides. Testing has shown that pesticide levels in rivers are often higher in cities than in agricultural areas. We have made progress along the road toward wiser pesticide use, but there is still far to go.

FOR DISCUSSION AND REFLECTION
Reducing our use of pesticides would likely change the character of the food we find in the supermarket. How would you feel about less perfect-looking food, like spottier apples?

faith connection

The land is an important theme throughout the Bible, and this theme provides some clues into the character of the relationship humans are to have with creation and with God. In the Bible, land is a sign of God's blessing and enduring care for God's people. As such, it is vitally important to the covenant which God makes with Abraham (Gen. 12:1-7) and with the Israelites fleeing from slavery in Egypt (Exod. 3:7-10). Land is also a dangerous temptation, however, because landedness gives the people a security independent from God's provision and may lead them to forget about God. It may also lead them into greed and a desire for earthly riches, which Jesus warns are sure ways of losing all that you have, both on earth and in heaven (Luke 12:13-21). Land is a symbol of faithfulness: God's faithfulness is expressed through the gift of land, and God's people's faithfulness is demonstrated through their treatment of the land.

(Adapted from S. Roy Kaufman)

FOR DISCUSSION AND REFLECTION

What does "land" mean to you today? Is it a gift? What tempts you to forget your dependence on God?

for meditation

For the Lord your God
is bringing you
into a good land,

a land
of flowing streams,
with springs and underground waters
welling up in valleys and hills,
a land of wheat and barley,
of vines and fig trees and pomegranates,
a land of olive trees and honey,
a land where you may eat bread without scarcity,
where you will lack nothing,
a land whose stones are iron
and from whose hills you may mine copper.

You shall eat your fill
and bless the Lord your God
for the good land
he has given you.

—Deuteronomy 8:7-11

for action

make insect repellent from vinegar, basil oil, lime juice, or mugwort oil. Avoid wearing scented soaps, perfumes and colognes during mosquito season.

learn to live with bugs—many insects are beneficial to both humans and the environment.

Remove weeds **by hand.**

Instead of covering your lawn with dangerous pesticides, **make a dandelion salad** (but make sure the dandelions haven't been sprayed first).

attract birds with bird feeders, bird baths, and bird houses—birds provide natural insect control.

Find an edible and medicinal plant book and **learn about the nutritional and curative properties** of "weeds" that grow in your area.

repel mosquitoes and flies by planting basil outside windows and doors.

plant marigolds, chrysanthemums, chives, onions, garlic, basil, savoury, horseradish, mint, or thyme among your garden plants. Their natural odours and root secretions repel some insects.

avoid using chemical pesticides on your lawn—instead try alternative weed killers, such as vinegar and water, insecticidal soap, and diatomaceous earth (a naturally occurring powder composed of the fossilized skeletons from marine and fresh water organisms).

WEEK 5

earth connection biotechnology: solving world hunger or frankenfood

According to estimates by the World Health Organization, about 500,000 children go blind from vitamin A deficiencies every year. Biotechnology has a solution: golden rice. This rice has been engineered to contain beta-carotene, the dietary source of vitamin A. Biotechnology supporters hail this achievement as proof that genetic engineering will save the world from hunger. Critics are doubtful, pointing out that a child would have to eat 9 kilograms of this rice per day to get the minimum daily requirement of vitamin A. Is biotechnology the answer to the world's food problems, or is it a dangerous technology threatening to destroy the environment and our health?

potential benefits of biotechnology

- less need for pesticides and other chemical inputs with crops that contain insecticides or are resistant to herbicides
- increased productivity
- improved food quality through nutrient enhancement
- disease prevention by inserting vaccines into regular foods
- potential to help clean up oil spills and other pollutants in fragile environments with bioengineered organisms

potential problems

- health risks to humans and animals, such as the transfer of toxins or allergenic compounds into new foods, or the creation of new toxins
- risks to the environment, such as the development of more aggressive weeds and the loss of biodiversity
- economic feasibility—development of genetic engineering is very costly

- property rights and patents raise moral questions over patenting life forms and make seeds more expensive and inaccessible
- getting the benefits to those who need them—profit-driven corporations will create products for those who can pay for them, not for those who are in the most desperate need
- concentration of power over the world's food in the hands of a few huge corporations

some facts about biotechnology

In 2001:

- 44.2 million hectares worldwide were cultivated with GMOs (genetically modified organisms)
- 75 percent of this total was in the global North
- the four major GMO crops are soybeans, maize, cotton, and canola
- the two major traits for which crops were engineered are insect resistance and herbicide tolerance.

Biotechnology is so new that the extent of both its benefits and its consequences are still largely unknown. More experimentation and more time is required to answer these questions. In the meantime, proceeding with caution is likely the most prudent response.

FOR DISCUSSION AND REFLECTION

Do you think biotechnology is a miracle of science, a dangerous technology, or something in between?

faith connection

The land theme also informs the human relationship with God and creation through the land tenure laws of the Old Testament. These are the most explicit and specific instructions given in the Bible for how humans are to be stewards in creation. The first principle of the land tenure policy is that the land belongs to God and the people are simply tenants (Lev. 25:23-24). As tenants, the Israelites are instructed to care for the land so that its bounty endures for many generations. They are also instructed to ensure that its bounty is made available to all peoples: the land and its produce must be shared equitably among all the people, with special provisions for the underprivileged—the widow, the orphan and the alien (Lev. 19:9-10; Deut. 14:28-29). The Sabbatical Provisions, which call for a day of rest on the seventh day (Exod. 20:8-11) and for the land to be left fallow during the seventh year (Exod. 23:10-11), further provide for the needs of the poor while reminding the people that it is through God that their needs are met and not by their own efforts. Faithful tenure of God's land involves both caring for the health of the land and ensuring the just distribution of its bounty. (*Adapted from S. Roy Kaufman*)

FOR DISCUSSION AND REFLECTION

What are some modern applications of the Old Testament land tenure laws? Is it possible to apply these principles within today's agricultural system? How might these laws be applied to modern city life?

for meditation

You shall observe my statutes
and faithfully keep my ordinances,
so that you may live
on the land securely.

The land will yield its fruit,
and you will eat your fill
and live on it securely.

Should you ask,
What shall we eat in the seventh year,
if we may not sow or gather in our crop?
I will order my blessing for you in the sixth year,
so that it will yield a crop for three years.
When you sow in the eighth year,
you will be eating from the old crop;
until the ninth year,
when its produce comes in,
you shall eat the old.

The land shall not be sold in perpetuity,
for the land is mine;
with me you are but aliens and tenants.

Throughout the land that you hold,
you shall provide
for the redemption of the land.

—Leviticus 25:18-24

for action

Avoid **wasting** food.

Remember to **give thanks** for every meal.

eat less meat —try substituting beans, nuts, and textured vegetable protein. Meat takes more land and energy to produce than vegetable sources of protein.

Avoid eating **highly processed food.**

write a letter to your elected representative asking for labelling of products containing GMOs and stricter legislation governing the introduction and use of new GMO products.

cook together with friends; then eat together.

Know what you are eating— **read labels.**

WEEK 6
earth connection

In 1989, Cuba was faced with a severe food crisis. The Soviet Union had collapsed and with it went Cuba's export market for its sugar and tobacco, as well as its source of petroleum, farm equipment, and food subsidies. Out of desperation, Cuba reverted to organic farming techniques, featuring small farms, urban gardens, and few mechanized or chemical inputs. Today, Cuba is a model of sustainable food production. Many of its cities produce almost all of their own food, and nutritious fresh fruits and vegetables are available to almost all citizens.

Proponents of biotechnology and industrialized farming argue that the world's growing food needs cannot be met except through large corporate farms using the newest and fanciest technology. However, high input industrialized farming is killing the family farm, exposing the public to potentially dangerous chemical residue on their food, and systematically degrading the land through overuse. Examples like Cuba suggest that there may be alternatives which are better for farmers, consumers, and the environment. Sustainable techniques may actually be more efficient in producing food and have the potential to empower small, family farmers around the world.

Organic farming is the most well-known alternative to conventional industrial-style farming, but it is not the only alternative, nor is it always a guarantee of sustainability. Sustainable agriculture is defined as an approach which seeks to produce food in ways which benefit the environment, the farmer, the community, and the consumer. It is accomplished by using and mimicking natural processes while avoiding nonrenewable and synthetic inputs. It requires local knowledge and community cooperation. Some examples of sustainable agriculture techniques include:

- intercropping: planting more than one variety or type of crop in the same plot to reduce pest problems and weather damage
- integrated pest management: the combination of biological methods like natural predators, cultural controls (such as vacuuming up insects), natural pesticides and bacterial and viral pesticides, and the limited use of a variety of chemicals to reduce pests to an economically acceptable level
- organic fertilizers, such as compost and manure
- water conservation
- efficient irrigation, such as drip irrigation which deposits the water right at the base of the plant instead of spraying it through the air
- crop rotation to improve the nutrient content of the soil
- soil conservation, through the use of conservation tillage, terracing, contour farming, strip cropping, mulches, cover crops, and silt traps
- integrated plant nutrition using livestock manures, composts, and legumes
- agroforestry—growing food crops and trees together.

FOR DISCUSSION AND REFLECTION

Many sustainable agriculture techniques require more labour than industrialized farming does. In an age of declining farm families and growing cities, how could such a system fit into our society? How might it affect women? Young people? Rural communities?

faith connection

As beings created in God's image, we are, in a certain sense, God's representatives on Earth. God is the Creator, and therefore, part of the human role in the world is to partake in the creation process. This task began with Adam naming the animals (Gen. 2:20) and is expressed in a great range of human activities, from worship, to technological innovations, to the arts. Like other special human abilities, our creativity sometimes leads us astray, but it is also our greatest tool in solving many of our problems and a special way in which we can connect to God.

FOR DISCUSSION AND REFLECTION

What are some examples of human creativity contributing to good stewardship?

for meditation

Be a gardener.
Dig a ditch,
toil and sweat,
and turn the earth upside down
and seek the deepness
and water the plants in time.
Continue this labor
and make sweet floods to run
and noble and abundant fruits
to spring.
Take this food and drink
and carry it to God
as your true worship.

— Julian of Norwich

for action

Educate yourself about **where your food comes from** and how it is produced.

If you live in an apartment or don't have a backyard, **get a vermi- compost** (a compost system using worms that can be done in a plastic tub inside).

compost— encourage your local government to set up a community composting program.

buy fresh, local, organic produce and products as often as possible (see http://eatwellguide.org for ideas). Visit the local farmer's market.

plant fruit or nut trees.

Pressure your local grocery store or cafeteria to provide **organic food.**

grow your own food in your backyard or in a community garden.

Cook using **simply in season**, the new MCC cookbook (available in the summer of 2005).

thinking long term

We have a yard and a small garden. The earth is the stuff that's timeless for me. It's been around a lot longer than I have, so I show some respect. I try to stay away from pesticides and herbicides so the dandelions are more numerous on my yard than on my neighbors'. But the rabbits feel welcome. I also choose not to grow potatoes if I don't feel up to handpicking the beetles. I plant apple tree varieties that are less prone to infestations so that I don't have to spray them to get a crop. These are little things, but they are indicative of an attitude. I try to think long-term when I make decisions about the patch of earth I live on.

—*7-Days trek participant*

marvelous compost

A seven year old visited our home last fall. He wanted to explore the yard and, above all, visit the compost heap to see what was in it. It was fascinating to watch him identify and marvel over the variety of kitchen scraps that had accumulated over the summer. I am often pessimistic about the future of civilization on this planet, but his love of the "earth" rekindles my hope.—*7-Days trek participant*

gambling with the sun . . .

Day 4: **gambling with the sun**

"We are embarked on the most colossal ecological experiment of all time—doubling the concentration in the atmosphere of an entire planet of one of its most important gases—and we really have little idea of what might happen."—Paul A. Colinvaux

Climate change is one of the most discussed and least understood of all environmental issues. Day 4 discusses what climate change is: its causes and how it can be expected to affect our planet. The Faith Connections in Day 4 explore how human beings are intimately a part of creation.

"And God said, 'Let there be lights in the dome of the sky to separate the day from the night; and let them be for signs and for seasons and for days and years, and let them be lights in the dome of the sky to give light upon the earth.' And it was so. God made two great lights—the greater light to rule the day and the lesser light to rule the night—and the stars. God set them in the dome of the sky to give light upon the earth, to rule over the day and over the night, and to separate the light from the darkness. And God saw that it was good. And there was evening and there was morning, the fourth day."

—Genesis 1:14-19

WEEK 1
earth connection

Climate change is an issue which has gotten a lot of press over the last couple of years, but is often still largely misunderstood, partly because even scientists remain uncertain about many things. So here are the facts, to the extent that they are known.

what is the greenhouse effect?

The Earth's atmosphere is made up of a combination of gases, including oxygen (21 percent), nitrogen (78 percent), and carbon dioxide (0.035 percent). When the radiation from the sun reaches Earth's atmosphere, most of it is either reflected back into space or absorbed by gases in the atmosphere. The radiation that reaches the Earth's surface is absorbed by the oceans and the land and is then reemitted as heat. Some of this heat escapes back out into space, but a large proportion is trapped by certain gases in the lower atmosphere (such as carbon dioxide, water vapour, and methane) and reradiated back to the Earth's surface. A similar effect occurs in a greenhouse or in a car on a sunny day. The glass allows the light from the sun to pass through, but traps it when it tries to escape in the form of heat. The greenhouse effect has become something we fear, but it is actually one of the factors that makes life on Earth possible. Without the greenhouse effect, the average surface temperature on the planet would be -19°C and the Earth would be a great ball of ice.

global climate change and its consequences

The composition of the gases in the atmosphere is balanced, ensuring that the proper amounts of energy enter and leave Earth's system to maintain the optimum temperature. During the last two centuries, however, human activities have altered that balance. We have been releasing large amounts of carbon dioxide and other greenhouse gases into the atmosphere and it is feared that the balance will be destroyed. According to scientific estimates, average global temperatures could increase by between 1°C to 3.5°C during the next century, and the annual mean temperatures in Canada could rise by 5°C to 10°C. For this reason, the consequences of the enhanced atmospheric greenhouse effect were originally called "global warming," but scientist soon realized that the effects would be much more complex than simply heating up the planet, so the term "global climate change" has been adopted.

activities which release greenhouse gases into the atmosphere

- burning of fossil fuels, such as coal and petroleum. Fossil fuels are used for industry, transportation and heating
- deforestation—carbon dioxide is released into the atmosphere when trees are burned. At the same time, living trees remove carbon dioxide from the atmosphere and this process is slowed when forests are destroyed
- use of chemical fertilizers which release nitrogen oxide
- release of CFCs (which also destroy the stratospheric ozone layer) from aerosol spray cans, old refrigerators, and air conditioners
- decomposition of organic materials in oxygen-free environments (such as a landfill, a cow's intestines, or underwater) which releases methane
- volcanic eruptions.

potential consequences of global climate change

- heating of the climate in some regions and cooling in others
- rising sea levels due to melting ice
- changes in precipitation patterns, affecting the availability and quality of fresh water

- increases in the frequency and intensity of extreme weather events
- flooding, drought, and extreme summer heat
- changes in habitat range and the possible extinction of some plants and animals
- increases in the number of heat-related illnesses and deaths
- increases in the range of tropical diseases
- decreases in agricultural productivity in tropical and subtropical regions (where the world's poorest people live) and increases in agricultural productivity in northern regions
- disruption of the ocean currents which move heat around the globe, causing major cooling in Europe and warming in the tropics
- human displacement and environmental refugees.

is the global climate really changing?

The evidence:

- the concentration of carbon dioxide in the lower atmosphere is at its highest in 420,000 years and it is still rising
- the 20th century was the hottest in the last 600 years
- the 1980s and 1990s were the warmest decades yet recorded
- 1998, 1997, 1995, 1990, and 1999 were the hottest years on record since 1860
- since 1860, the average global temperature of surface air has risen by 0.6-0.7°C. Most of this increase has occurred since 1946.
- the incidence of extreme weather events has increased by 28 percent since 1975.

Global climate change is a contentious issue both politically and scientifically. While it is an observable fact that greenhouse gas levels in the environment are increasing and at an unprecedented speed, it is difficult for scientists to make specific and accurate predictions about what might happen. There are so many different factors that affect the global climate, from variations in solar radiation and the tilt and orbit of the planet, to long-term climactic cycles which have caused both ice ages and warm periods throughout the history of the planet. Many of these factors are part of cycles with thousand-year time ranges. It is therefore difficult to guess the result of the interactions of these many factors over time.

Because there is disagreement and uncertainty within the scientific community, and because counteracting global climate change will probably require drastic changes to our society and way of life, many people choose to believe that the predictions are grossly over-exaggerated or that new technology will prevent a global disaster. But whether the worst-case scenarios put out by scientists are true or not is, perhaps, not the most important question. A more relevant question may be how profoundly we should alter and change the global system, regardless of how it may affect our lives or those of our children.

(Statistics from www.climatechange.gc.ca; Katie Alvord, Divorce Your Car: Ending the Love Affair with the Automobile *[Gabriola Island, B.C.: New Society Publishers, 2000], 70-71; and G. Tyler Miller,* Sustaining the Earth, *5th ed. [Belmont, Calif.: Brooks/Cole Thomson Learning, 2002], 260.)*

Do you believe that climate change is a serious threat?

faith connection

Recognizing the special role that human beings play in creation is important, but focussing solely on human distinctiveness leads dangerously close to the anthropocentric attitudes which have largely been responsible for our destructive behaviour toward the Earth. While human beings are unquestionably unique, we are still fundamentally a part of creation. Adam, the first man, was formed from the dust of the ground (Gen. 2:7); in fact, his name is derived from the Hebrew word for soil. In the Genesis 1 account of creation, humans are created on the same day as the land animals, further evidence of our closeness to the rest of creation. Like other creatures, we depend on the fruits of the Earth for all our needs and desires; we may alter them drastically before using them, but everything that we use and make comes from the Earth—even plastic was once a prehistoric fish. Furthermore, human beings share the mortal destiny of all living creatures, and shall, in the end, return to dust (Gen. 3:19). These connections to the rest of creation forge a kinship between all creatures. The birds, animals, trees, mountains, and rivers are, in a sense, our brothers and sisters.

FOR DISCUSSION AND REFLECTION
How do you experience your kinship or interdependence with the rest of the world?

for meditation

We are the earth, through the plants and animals that nourish us.
We are the rains and the oceans that flow through our veins.
We are the breath of the forests of the land, and the plants of the sea.
We are human animals, related to all other life as descendants of the firstborn cell.
We share with these kin a common history, written in our genes.
We share a common present, filled with uncertainty.
And we share a common future, as yet untold.

—David Suzuki Foundation

for action

turn off lights, appliances, televisions, and computers when they are not needed.

install solar panels for heating and/or hot water.

plant trees— trees absorb carbon dioxide from the atmosphere and store it.

check out more hints for increasing the energy efficiency of your home at http://oee.nrcan.gc.ca/houses-maisons/english/homeowners/whyenerguide/whyenerguide.cfm.

WEEK 2
earth connection victims of climate change: the tropics

Coral reefs are some of the most vibrant and diverse ecosystems on the planet. The brightly coloured reefs are formed by a collaboration between coral animals that build the reef and microscopic algae that capture sunlight and turn it into food. These reefs house a whole host of fish and other marine creatures that coexist in complex and fascinating relationships. One type of fish, for example, serves as a toothbrush for larger fish, swimming into their mouths and removing dangerous bacteria. Coral reefs are important to humans because their beauty and diversity make them popular for tourists, and they also supply food and natural chemicals that can be used for medicine.

Unfortunately, many of the world's coral reefs are dying. Scientists are not certain why, but they suspect that increases in water temperature have put stress on this complex system. With a rise in temperature of as little as 1°C above the monthly summer average, the coral can become more susceptible to parasites and disease. Heat stress also causes them to expel the algae upon which they rely for nutrients. The Australian Institute of Marine Science predicts that climate change may cause ocean temperatures to rise from 1.5-4.5°C, which would devastate the world's coral.

Warming of the ocean's temperature is also harmful to human populations. In 2001, the leaders of Tuvalu, a small island nation in the Pacific Ocean, announced that its citizens will have to abandon their homeland because of rising sea levels. These changes in sea levels are attributed to increased global temperatures which have caused glaciers to melt and ocean waters to expand in volume.

The people of Tuvalu are not alone in their fate. As sea levels are projected to rise by as much as a metre during this century, hundreds of millions of people in coastal areas around the world will be affected. Densely populated countries such as Bangladesh, India, Indonesia and China are particularly at risk and there is the potential for massive migrations of environmental refugees. The 11,000 citizens of Tuvalu are struggling to find a place to relocate—where will the hundreds of millions go?

FOR DISCUSSION AND REFLECTION

Climate change, and other environmental disasters, have the potential to exponentially increase the number of refugees in the world. What are the implications of this increase in displaced peoples for world security? How will this affect individual countries—the countries that are experiencing the environmental disasters and the countries that are potential havens for the refugees?

faith connection

"He said to him, 'You shall love the Lord your God with all your heart, and with all your soul, and with all your mind. This is the greatest and first commandment. And a second is like it: You shall love your neighbour as yourself. On these two commandments hang all the law and the prophets.'"—Matthew 22:34-40

St. Francis of Assisi was a medieval monk and mystic who perceived God's presence in everything. He was keenly aware of his creaturehood and the kinship which exists between humans and other creatures. He had a deep affection and regard for all living things and sought to build unity between God and all creatures. According to legend, St. Francis had a special connection with animals and other natural elements that allowed him to communicate with them. For instance, he is said to have tamed a man-eating wolf. He also preached to birds, exhorting them to love and praise God. St. Francis considered all creatures to be his sisters and brothers and loved them as he loved himself. In 1979, he was declared the patron saint of the environment.

FOR DISCUSSION AND REFLECTION

How do you experience your kinship or interdependence with the rest of creation? Would you consider the sun as your brother or the moon as your sister?

for meditation
canticle of the sun (excerpts)

All praise be yours, my Lord through all that you have made,
  And first my lord Brother Sun,
  Who brings the day; and light you give to us
  through him.

How beautiful is he, how radiant in all his splendor!
  Of you, Most High, he bears the likeness.

All praise be yours, my Lord, through Sister moon and Stars;
  In the heavens you have made them, bright
  And precious and fair.

All praise be yours, my Lord, through Brothers Wind and Air,
  And fair and stormy, all the weather's moods,
  By which you cherish all that you have made.

All praise be yours, my Lord, through Sister Water,
so useful, lowly, precious, and pure.

All praise be yours, my Lord, through Brother Fire,
Through whom you brighten up the night.
How beautiful he is, how joyful! Full of power and strength.

All praise be yours, my Lord, through Sister Earth, our mother,
Who feeds us in her sovereignty and produces
Various fruits and colored flowers and herbs.

Praise and bless my Lord, and give him thanks,
And serve him with great humility.

—St. Francis

turn thermostat down
when you are not in the house or when you are sleeping—install a programmable thermostat to do this automatically.

seal leaks
around doors, windows and cracks where heat can escape.

insulate
your home.

for action

When buying new appliances and vehicles, choose the most energy-efficient model. Check for the **EnerGuide label.**

clean furnace filters and keep furnace properly tuned.

WEEK 3
earth connection victims of climate change: the arctic

In the growing spring light, an Inuit hunter is tracking a seal across the Arctic sea ice. Periodically, he checks the ice to make sure it is safe. Often he has to change his course because the ice is soft—too soft for so early in the Arctic spring. Centuries of accumulated knowledge and experience have given this hunter and his people an intimate knowledge of the harsh landscape in which they have learned to survive. But in recent years, the climate has been changing, altering the landscape and the creatures that live on it.

It is expected that the changes brought by global climate change will be greater and more rapid in the polar regions than in any other region of the planet. Some of these changes are already occurring. Fall freeze-up is arriving up to a month later than usual and spring thaw also comes earlier. Sea ice has decreased, making it harder for Inuit communities to access the seals which constitute the major part of their traditional diet. Changes in sea ice also make travel more difficult.

The Arctic is almost entirely underlain by permafrost, which is also beginning to melt. This causes the land to slump and collapse along coastlines, lake shores, and underneath buildings. Further thawing could endanger roads, buildings, bridges, and oil pipelines.

A whole host of new species are also appearing in the Arctic, including new birds, new fish, and more flies and mosquitoes. Warmer temperatures may also bring in bacteria which could contaminate drinking water. At the same time, animals and plants which have adapted to the conditions of the Arctic may suffer. There is particular concern about polar bears, who depend on sea ice to access their food.

The Arctic is one of the few places left on the Earth that has not been profoundly altered by human culture and technology. Global climate change may end this legacy.

faith connection

The connection that the Inuit hunter has with the land goes deeper than simply a practical need to understand the environment from which he gets his food. Like the people in many Aboriginal cultures around the world, his connection to the land is also fundamentally spiritual. People who still live close to the land, and depend on it directly for their daily needs, have a profound sense of their place in creation which is cemented into their religious understanding. At the centre of this understanding is a deep respect for the Creator, which then extends to all that the Creator has made. The closeness of God to creation makes every part of the Earth sacred, and makes the people responsible to honour it and to protect it. The general attitude that flows from these beliefs is one ". . . of acceptance, of appreciating the land as it is, of accommodating one's self to the land, of blending in with it" (Anne W. Rowthorn).

FOR DISCUSSION AND REFLECTION

The First Nations people of North America have much wisdom in their traditions about caring for the land and the Earth. How do other cultures and faith contribute insight toward faithful stewardship of creation?

for meditation

"We should understand well that all things are the works of the Great Spirit. We know that he is within all things: the trees, the grasses, the rivers, the mountains, and all the four-legged animals and the winged peoples . . . and even more important, we should understand that he is above all these things and peoples. When we do understand all this deeply in our hearts, then we will fear and love, and know the Great Spirit, and then we will be and act and live as he intends."—Black Elk

for action

Buy food and other products that are **grown or manufactured locally** to cut down on transportation needs.

write a letter to your elected representative expressing your concern about climate change and your support for climate change prevention legislation, such as the Kyoto Protocol.

Reverence, repair, reduce, reuse and recycle—manufacturing and transporting new products creates greenhouse gases. **The five r's reduce our need for new products.**

WEEK 4
earth connection

How many hours did you spend in a car today? What about this week? Or this month? Average Canadians travel about 20,000 kilometres a year, mostly in cars, light trucks or minivans. Cars and light trucks account for 56 percent of greenhouse gas emissions from transportation in Canada. Transportation contributes to 25 percent of that country's greenhouse gas emissions, making it the single largest source of greenhouse gas emissions.

For the last century, Canadians and Americans have had an enduring love affair with the automobile. A car is more than just a practical way to get around; it is a coming of age ritual, a sign of status in society, and a symbol of freedom and independence. But our relationship with cars is not a healthy one. Automobiles spew large amounts of pollutants into the air, and in addition to their contribution to the greenhouse effect, these pollutants also cause respiratory problems for many people. At the same time, the large amount of time spent sitting in the car has contributed to widespread obesity among Canadians and Americans. Automobiles also force cities to devote large tracts of land to roadways and parking lots and encourage urban sprawl. This becomes a vicious cycle, as sprawling cities become impossible to navigate by any other means than the automobile.

Reducing car usage is one of the biggest steps that individuals can take to slow climate change. This means pulling out your walking shoes, your bicycle, or your bus tickets. It also means pressuring your municipal government to invest in public transit and to take steps to stop urban sprawl.

(Statistics from Power Shift: Cool Solutions to Global Warming, *David Suzuki Foundation; Transport Canada, http://www.tc.gc.ca/programs/environment/climate*

change/menu.htm; Environment Canada, http://www.ec.gc.ca/eco/transport/cli-mate_e.html)

FOR DISCUSSION AND REFLECTION

Can you imagine living without a car? How would you have to adapt your daily routine? If you don't have a car, what do you do to get around?

faith connection

*"You have heard that it was said, 'You shall love your neighbor and hate your enemy.'
But I say to you, Love your enemies and pray for those who persecute you."*
—Matthew 5:43-44a

People in western cultures have long viewed nature, or at least elements of nature, as an enemy. The natural world has been seen as a place of chaos, disorder, and evil which needed to be tame and civilized. This taming process has often been violent and destructive. It has also been understood as a holy obligation. In light of the above Scripture passage, this adversarial attitude should perhaps be reevaluated. In the twenty-first century, we no longer fear the woods or the wilds the way that our pioneering ancestors often did, but we still try to wage war against natural forces which disrupt our lives and damage our possessions. Like most wars, this generally makes the situation worse.

The wild fires which ravaged many communities in British Columbia and California in the summer of 2003 are one example of a desperate battle against the forces of nature. Other evidence of war we wage against nature can be seen through the windows of the Mennonite Central Committee Winnipeg office, where a large earthen dike has been constructed to protect nearby homes and businesses from the regular flooding of the Red River.

The typical response to events like flooding and fires, inspired in part by our desire to subdue nature, is to suppress or even stop them. But fires are necessary to the life of a forest, and floods renew the nutrients of the land. As members of the created world, human beings share in these benefits. Our attempts to change or stop them not only suppress these benefits but also bring greater pain to us. Forest fires burn hotter and more dangerously if they do not occur regularly, and dikes and dams often make flood damages worse. Making peace with the natural world, and learning to love our "enemies" in nature, means accepting our place in creation and adapting to the natural processes that occur.

FOR DISCUSSION AND REFLECTION

What natural "enemies" exist in your region? How could you apply peace principles in your response to these enemies?

for meditation

We live by the sun
We feel by the moon
We move by the stars

We live in all things
all things live in us

We eat from the earth
We drink from the rain
We breathe of the air

We live in all things
All things live in us

We call to each other
We listen to each other
Our hearts deepen with love
and compassion

We live in all things
All things live in us

We depend on the trees
and animals
We depend on the earth
Our minds open with wisdom
and insight

We live in all things
All things live in us

We dedicate our practice to others
We include all forms of life
We celebrate the joy of living-dying

We live in all things
All things live in us

We are full of life
We are full of death
We are grateful for all beings and
companions

—Stephanie Kaza

for action

Plan a **"car fast"** for several days—invite others to join you.

Write to car companies demanding **better fuel efficiency.**

Read Katie Alvord, *divorce your car: ending the love affair with the automobile.* New Society Publishers, 2000.

Share rides with others as often as possible.

Encourage your local government to provide **better public transit** service and bicycle facilities.

Consider buying a **hybrid** (gas/electric engine) car.

walk or bike for short trips and take public transit or carpool for longer trips.

Check out the **what would jesus drive** campaign and sign the pledge www.whatwouldjesusdrive.org.

drive at moderate speeds (eg. 90 km/h or 55 miles/h on the highway) to save energy and reduce pollution.

figure out approximately how many kilometres/miles you drove in the last year. Use your car's average fuel efficiency to figure out how many kilograms/pounds of carbon dioxide you released into the atmosphere during this time.

Make sure your car is **serviced regularly.**

Devise a plan for getting where you need to go that would **reduce your carbon dioxide** emissions by 75 percent. Follow this plan for a week. Consider extending it for a longer period of time.

If you are moving, try to **choose a home** within a 30 minute walk, bike, or transit ride from your work or school.

avoid idling your vehicle—idling uses more fuel than restarting your engine.

avoid carrying heavy things in your car—extra weight causes the car to burn more fuel.

When buying a new car, buy the **smallest model** that will meet your needs.

Organize a **carpooling program** at your church, school, or workplace.

quiet time for the soul

Creation remains unbounded by human "progress." Here in Winnipeg, I have recently discovered the joys of cross-country skiing, and am exploring the river-banks, trees, and even sidewalks of my area. Last weekend, I went out by the river and my soul was quieted by large flakes that seemed to muffle everything. But this feeling did not stop when I once again returned to the populated streets. We often overlook the natural urban havens in our rush to "get away." Perhaps this process is more internal than we acknowledge.—*7-Days trek participant*

all creatures . . .

 Day 5: **all creatures**

"For one species to mourn the death of another is a new thing under the sun. The Cro-Magnon who slew the last mammoth thought only of steaks. The sportsman who shot the last pigeon thought only of his prowess. The sailor who clubbed the last auk thought of nothing at all. But we, who have lost our pigeons, mourn the loss. Had the funeral been ours, the pigeon would hardly have mourned us."—Aldo Leopold

the last passenger pigeon, a species which used to fill the skies of North America in multitudes, died at the Cincinnati Zoological Garden in 1914. This is but one of many species which have been disappearing at an unprecedented rate during the last century. While experts estimate that five or six mass extinctions have occurred in the past, the mass extinction that is facing the planet today is artificially induced by human activity. Day 5 explores the types of human activity which are causing this accelerated rate of extinction, and measures that are being taken to save the Earth's diversity. Day 5 also discusses the implications of salvation for creation.

"And God said, 'Let the water bring forth swarms of living creatures, and let birds fly above the earth across the dome of the sky.' So God created the great sea monsters and every living creature that moves, of every kind, with which the waters swarm, and every winged bird of every kind. And God saw that it was good. God blessed them saying, 'Be fruitful and multiply and fill the waters in the seas, and let birds multiply on the earth.' And there was evening and there was morning, the fifth day."
—Genesis 1:20-23

WEEK 1
earth connection

The island of Singapore is haunted by the living dead. They aren't dead yet, but they will be soon. The living dead is the term that ecologists are using for a number of species in Southeast Asia which have such low populations that they are doomed for extinction. The cause is habitat destruction. During the last 200 years, over 95 percent of Singapore's forest cover and freshwater habitats have disappeared due to urbanization, agriculture, and logging, and ecologists estimate that 28 percent of its species diversity has already been lost. Based on the situation in Singapore, ecologists fear that 20 percent of the Earth's plant and animal species may disappear within the next hundred years.

To the northeast of Singapore, another Asian island is celebrating its species diversity through new conservation efforts. Taiwan's Fuyuan Forest Resort is a bird watcher's paradise. It features lush rainforest, fifty different bird species, and rare butterflies. Awareness programs have curbed the local practice of hunting these birds for food and catching the butterflies for decoration. Other activities that are destructive to the forest habitat, such as dumping industrial waste, gravel digging in river beds, and using electric wires to catch fish, have also been stopped. The vibrant beauty and exotic diversity of this small park is attracting bird watchers from around the world, allowing the Taiwanese to support themselves and protect their natural heritage at the same time.

The contrasting examples of Singapore and Taiwan illustrate the ongoing battle to balance human needs and those of the animals, birds, and fish with whom we share this planet. The growth of human civilization has inexorably expanded into the wild, natural places that sustain many of the Earth's creatures. While finding food, water, and shelter is necessary for human survival, maintaining the diversity of life on the planet is necessary for the survival of everything on Earth, including humans.

why is diversity important?

Biological diversity, or biodiversity, refers to the wide variety of different species which live on this planet. The extent of the Earth's diversity is not entirely known, but scientists estimate that there may be as many as 100 million different species. So far, only 1.8 million of these have been identified and named. These numbers are staggering, and make one wonder why the Earth needs so many different species.

- Biodiversity is one of the pillars upon which the natural world stands. All the creatures living within a certain habitat, or ecosystem, interact with each other in complex ways. The wide variety of different creatures and their mutual interrelations make all their lives possible. When one species disappears, the entire system is disrupted and other species are harmed as well. Biodiversity is as important as water to drink and air to breathe.

- Biodiversity also serves as an insurance system. If the environment changes, if one species disappears, or if there is a natural disaster, diversity both within the genetic make-up of individual species and within the community of living organisms as a whole, provides a greater chance that the community of living beings will be able to adapt to the new conditions.

(Statistics from Michael Hopkins, "Deforestation could wipe out one-fifth of species," Nature Science Update, *July 24, 2003. www.nature.com/nsu/nsu_pf/030721/ 030721-9.html; David Suzuki, "Living Dead Haunt Southeast Asia,"* Science

Matters, *August 1, 2003. www.davidsuzuki.org/about_us/Dr_David_Suzuki/Article_ Archives /weekly08010301.asp)*

FOR DISCUSSION AND REFLECTION

Why do human beings mourn the loss of other species? How do these species add to our lives?

faith connection

In the beginning of creation, all was well—with God, with humanity, with heaven and earth. Then Adam and Eve ate the forbidden fruit, the ground was cursed, and the people were banished from the garden. The harmony between God and people had been broken, and the harmony in creation as a whole was also marred. But God is a merciful God and graciously offers salvation and redemption to all of creation (Isa. 65:17-25; John 3:16). Just as humans yearn for a final transformation and the liberation from sin, so does the rest of creation wait with eager longing to be set free from its bondage (Rom. 8:18-23). When this transformation occurs, rivers will flow through the desert, trees will burst into blossom, and all that has become barren and destroyed will be renewed. It will be like a new Eden, the garden restored (Ezek. 36:33-36), and like in the garden, the Earth will joyfully pour forth its bounty. "The time is surely coming, says the Lord, when the one who plows shall overtake the one who reaps, and the treader of grapes the one who sows the seed; the mountains shall drip sweet wine, and all the hills shall flow with it" (Amos 9:13).

How do you respond to the idea of salvation encompassing not only humans, but all of creation? Is this a new idea for you?

for meditation
God's grandeur

The world is charged with the grandeur of God.
* It will flame out, like shining from shook foil;*
* It gathers to a greatness, like the ooze of oil*
Crushed. Why do men then not reck his rod?
Generations have trod, have trod, have trod;
And all is seared with trade; bleared, smeared with toil;
And wears man's smudge and shares man's smell: the soil
Is bare now, nor can feet feel, being shod.

And for all this, nature is never spent;
* There lives the dearest freshness deep down things;*
* And though the last lights off the black West went*
* Oh morning, at the brown brink eastward, springs—*
Because the Holy Ghost over the bent
World broods with warm breast and with ah! bright wings.

—Gerard Manley Hopkins

for action

create a butterfly or bird-friendly garden in your yard or on your balcony by planting native wildflowers, shrubs, and grasses.

Encourage public works and parks departments **not to mow roadsides**.

Support campaigns that **restrict logging** in provincial and national parks.

Read Douglas Adams and Mark Carwardine, *last chance to see.* London: Pan Books, 1990.

spend an afternoon with a bird watcher—learn the names of specific birds that visit your neighbourhood.

Choose products marked **rainforest-friendly.**

Use **biodegradable** cleaning and personal washing products where available.

become a member of a wildlife protection agency.

WEEK 2
earth connection

At a speed of 300 km/h, a small grey-brown streak plunges out of the prairie sky. It is a peregrine falcon in pursuit of lunch. Peregrine falcons are small predatory birds that are renowned for the great distances and speeds at which they can travel. Because of these abilities, they have long been prized by falconers for hunting game. The collection of chicks for falconry, however, contributed to the falcon's near brush with extinction in Canada during the early 1970s.

The most significant cause of the falcon's demise, however, was the use of agricultural pesticides like DDT. DDT is a chemical which breaks down very slowly. It is picked up by animals at the lower end of the food chain and passed on through various predators, increasing in concentration at each level. Animals at the top of the food chain, such as falcons, can accumulate levels of DDT up to a hundred times greater than their prey. The DDT causes eggs to form with thin shells, which prevents chicks from reaching maturity. Similar problems also threaten eagles and other predatory birds.

DDT was banned for use in Canada in 1972 (and in the United States in 1969). Peregrine falcons were placed on the endangered species list and aggressive programs were set in place to restore them. The combination of captive breeding and reintroduction programs has successfully brought the peregrine falcon back from the brink. In 1999, it was down-listed from "endangered" to "threatened" and by the year 2000, an estimated 500 breeding pairs were living in Canada. These birds are still at risk, however, due to their small population size and the diminishing quality of their habitat.

why are predators important?

All species play an important role in their ecosystems, but predators are considered to be especially important. They contribute to stability in living systems by ensuring that other species' populations do not grow beyond the capacity of the ecosystem to sustain them. Predators are more at risk than other species, however, because their populations tend to be smaller and because humans often see them as competition. For instance, wolf and coyote extermination programs have been undertaken to protect farm livestock and deer populations. In the case of deer, the wolves are actually essential to their survival. Without wolves, deer populations explode. This is usually followed by a population crash due to starvation as the burgeoning deer community denudes its food sources. Predators prevent these kinds of extreme vacillations in population and thereby ensure the health of the entire ecosystem.

faith connection

A frequent criticism of the Christian attitude toward nature is that Christians are so preoccupied with spiritual salvation that they care little for what occurs on Earth in the here and now. In the Bible, however, there are four different models of salvation:

this-worldly salvation is a concrete act which occurs in the present place and time.
- God provides wholeness of life, good harvests, fertility, absence of war, and shalom within the family in a continual way.
- God redirects human life on earth through periodic moments of transformation from injustice, oppression, and bondage to shalom, such as the Exodus and the return from the exile. (Found throughout the Old Testament.)

next-worldly salvation is a hope for future salvation.

- Often developing in times of oppression, biblical writers looked forward to a grand-scale transformation, through which God would create a new heaven and a new earth where righteousness, justice and shalom would reign.
- This is a salvation of recreation which involves the Earth and all its creatures. (Found in Isaiah, Jeremiah, Daniel, the intertestamental Jewish writings, the Gospels of Matthew, Mark, and Luke, the writings of Paul, and Revelation.)

salvation as monarchic unification is salvation through the unification of the heavenly realm and the earthly realm.

- Christ fills the whole earth—he is the agent of creation through whom the whole universe is reconciled.
- Salvation is spatial rather than temporal—time is irrelevant. (Found in Colossians and Ephesians.)

other-worldly salvation involves the departure of the spirit from this fallen world to the refuge of heaven.

- Salvation is very spiritual and spatial in nature.
- The Earth and its physical limitations are viewed as fallen and evil. (Found in the Gospel of John and Hebrews.)

These models reflect the various ways we experience God's salvation. Traditionally, Christians have emphasized other-worldly salvation to the exclusion of the other models. Unfortunately, this model has the least impetus for an environmental ethic because it is entirely spiritual and denies the importance and goodness of the physical creation. In light of the various facets of salvation exhibited by all four models, it is clear that salvation is both spiritual and physical, involves both heaven and earth, and includes all creation.

(Adapted from Gordon Zerbe)

FOR DISCUSSION AND REFLECTION

What do you think about the four different models of salvation? Which model is most meaningful to you?

for meditation

"I consider that the sufferings of this present time are not worth comparing with the glory about to be revealed to us. For the creation waits with eager longing for the revealing of the children of God; for the creation was subjected to futility, not of its own will but by the will of the one who subjected it, in hope that the creation itself will be set free from its bondage to decay and will obtain the freedom of the glory of the children of God. We know that the whole creation has been groaning in labor pains until now; and not only the creation, but we ourselves, who have the first fruits of the Spirit, groan inwardly while we wait for adoption, the redemption of our bodies."
—Romans 8:18-23

for action

Use **organic pest control** methods in your garden and on your yard.

find out what species are endangered in your region. Write a letter to your government urging it to take steps to protect these species.

eat less meat, or eat grass fed animals (these are usually organic)—most livestock are grain fed, which requires more land than raising grain for human consumption. Ranching in certain areas also destroys wild animal habitat.

WEEK 3
earth connection

The kakapo is probably the strangest bird in the whole world. It is a large, fat parrot that doesn't know how to fly and it booms. To attract a mate, the male kakapo digs himself a small bowl high in the mountains with which he makes a deep, powerful booming noise. The female will walk over thirty kilometres in one night to find a booming male, but only if she has had the right kind of fruit for breakfast. They are truly strange birds, and there were once hundreds of thousands of them in New Zealand. Today there are about eighty-six.

Before humans reached the islands of New Zealand, there were almost no mammals—only birds and reptiles. There were also no predators, and consequently, many of the birds lost the ability to fly. Kiwi birds and kakapos are two such examples. When humans arrived, first from Polynesia and then from Europe, they brought with them a number of predatory mammals, including rats, stoats, weasels, cats, and dogs, which immediately started to prey on the flightless birds. Kakapos are gentle creatures which have no concept of danger; they often don't even try to run away from an attacker. As one would suspect, they began to disappear very quickly.

The introduction of foreign species is very destructive to a living community and is referred to as biotic pollution. Exotic species can prey on indigenous species and compete with them for food and habitat. These species often do not have predators or other natural controls in their new habitat and so they can quickly take over, smothering all other species. Other examples are the introduction of rabbits to Australia, which caused increased desertification, and the zebra mussel, which entered the Great Lakes system of North America through the shipping industry, and has caused millions of dollars of damage by clogging up pipes and congregating on boats, docks, piers, and buoys.

FOR DISCUSSION AND REFLECTION

One of the measures being taken to save the kakapo is the creation of kakapo reserves on small islands off the south of New Zealand. On these reserves, all potential predators (like cats, rats, etc.) are exterminated. Do you think it is ethical to kill off some species of animal in certain areas to save another species from extinction?

faith connection

"I will make for you a covenant on that day with the wild animals, the birds of the air, and the creeping things of the ground; and I will abolish the bow, the sword, and war from the land; and I will make you lie down in safety."—Hosea 2:16-18

The redemption which is promised by God through the prophets and through the incarnation of Jesus is a promise of reconciliation. Sin not only separates people from God, but also from other people and from the rest of creation. The salvation of the world is a restoration of all these relationships, allowing all creatures to live in joyful communion with each other and with their Creator. Mennonite theology professes that as committed members of the body of Christ, we live as signs of the kingdom which has already broken into the world, and which will come in complete fullness in the future. What then is our role in demonstrating this transformation in our relationship to nature?

FOR DISCUSSION AND REFLECTION

How do you express signs of hope and renewal in your relationship with the rest of the created world?

for meditation
vision of the peaceable kingdom

The wolf shall live with the lamb,
* the leopard shall lie down with the kid,*
the calf and the lion and the fatling together,
* and a little child shall lead them.*
The cow and the bear shall graze,
* their young shall lie down together;*
* and the lion shall eat straw like the ox.*
The nursing child shall play over the hole of the asp,
* and the weaned child shall put its hand on the adder's den.*
They will not hurt or destroy
* on all my holy mountain;*
for the earth will be full of the knowledge of the Lord
* as the waters cover the sea.*

—Isaiah 11:6-9

for action

report poaching.

spay or neuter your cats and dogs
(unless you are using them for breeding) and don't let them wander to prevent them from preying on local wildlife.

when adopting pets,
investigate how the animals are obtained—the acquisition of many animal involves harmful practices, from puppy mills to removing endangered tropical fish from their natural habitat.

Avoid buying products which are made from **endangered or threatened species**,
such as furs, ivory products, items made of reptile skin, and tortoiseshell jewelry.

WEEK 4
earth connection

For centuries, the people of Newfoundland have lived on the bounty of the sea. The vast oceans, which cover most of the Earth's surface, used to seem limitless— until recently. In 1992, the northern cod stock had plummeted so low that the Canadian government imposed a moratorium on most of the cod fishery. In April 2003, the fishery was closed completely, probably forever. The cod will likely never come back.

The main reason for the collapse of the cod in the northern Atlantic is over- fishing. Modern technologies, from sonar and navigational gear, to huge nets, to factory ships, allow fishers to catch massive numbers of fish. It doesn't take long before the breeding stock is too small to maintain the species' numbers. When a fish species becomes commercially extinct, like the cod, it is no longer profitable to harvest it. Around 70 percent of the world's commercial fish stocks are reach- ing this point. Fortunately, fish become commercially extinct before they disap- pear altogether, so there is a chance to intervene. But as in the case of the Newfoundland cod, the ecosystem may be too altered by their diminished num- bers for the population ever to recover. And even if they do, the consequences in the meantime are grave, for both the people who lost their jobs and for the marine ecosystem. People often argue against environmental protection because they are afraid it will cost too much and hurt the economy, but this is a clear example of how failing to address environmental problems in time will mean more harm to both the economy and the environment in the long run.

Are caring for the environment and maintaining a healthy economy incompatible goals?

faith connection

The story of Jesus's birth at Christmas is the most basic of the Christian faith. The story of God's son, however, begins much earlier. Jesus Christ was with God in the very beginning (John 1:1) and participated in the creation of the world. Then, as an expression of love for that creation, he took on human flesh and became part of that creation to redeem it. Through his death and resurrection, the whole universe, "every creature under heaven" (Col.1:23), is saved, restored, and made new. Christ's incarnation is an affirmation of the goodness and sanctity of the material substance of the Earth and directly opposes the tendency to spiritualize salvation and ignore the welfare of the Earth.

"He is the image of the invisible God, the firstborn of all creation; for in him all things in heaven and on earth were created, things visible and invisible, whether thrones or dominions or rulers or powers—all things have been created through him and for him . . . For in him all the fullness of God was pleased to dwell, and through him God was pleased to reconcile to himself all things, whether on earth or in heaven, by making peace through the blood of his cross."—Colossians 1:15-20

FOR DISCUSSION AND REFLECTION
How do you respond to the idea that Jesus is the "firstborn of creation" and thereby saves, restores, and redeems all of creation?

for meditation

"The Redeemer could penetrate the stuff of the cosmos, could pour himself into the life-blood of the universe, only by first dissolving himself in matter, later to be reborn from it . . . It is because Christ was 'inoculated' in matter that he can no long be dissociated from the growth of Spirit; that he could henceforth be torn away from it only by rocking the foundations of the universe."—Teilhard deChardin

for action

buy dolphin-friendly tuna
—look for the label.

avoid eating cod
or other seafood that is threatened.

Avoid buying drinks with **plastic rings**, or cut the rings before throwing them away—animals can get entangled in them.

do not release helium balloons
into the air—they can choke marine animals such as turtles.

what did cod taste like?

I get so angry when I think about the collapse of the cod stocks. It was so obvious that this was coming. How could it not? The very means of catching the fish, drag nets, was destroying the spawning beds. Everyone who knew anything about the fishery knew this. But no one stopped it. There was denial upon denial. Temporary greed and "jobs for political ends" were the deciding factors. And it continues with other stocks in other oceans NOW. How will we respond to our grandchildren when they ask, "What did cod taste like? What was it like to catch a wild salmon on a rod? What was it like? What was it like to have your own boat to fish the Grand Banks? To have a real job where you worked for yourself, not for a paycheck in a big box store?" Sure we're into a world of "new economies," but are they better than the old? You can't eat electrons, and you can't live in a house built of software. This thought haunts me. Will my children or grandchildren some day ask: "When you were making your decisions about economies and the earth, didn't you care about me?"—7-*Days trek participant*

in God's image . . .

 Day 6: **in God's image...**

"History is governed by those overarching movements that give shape and meaning to life by relating the human venture to the larger destinies of the universe. Creating such a movement might be called the Great Work of a people . . . The Great Work now, as we move into a new millennium, is to carry out the transition from a period of human devastation of the Earth to a period when humans would be present to the planet in a mutually beneficial manner."—Thomas Berry

day 6 is an exploration of the human dimensions of the ecological dilemma, addressing various aspects of human behaviour and society which must be part of the Great Work envisioned by Thomas Berry. These include consumption, population, economics, technology, and urban life. Biblical correlations to these issues are also explored, particularly in the context of Jesus's ministry.

"Then God said, 'Let us make humankind in our image, according to our likeness; and let them have dominion over the fish of the sea, and over the birds of the air, and over the cattle, and over all the wild animals of the earth, and over every creeping thing that creeps upon the earth.'"

—Genesis 1:26

WEEK 1
earth connection

In the year 2000, 20 percent of the world's population
- had 85 percent of the world's wealth and income
- used 88 percent the world's natural resources
- generated 75 percent of the world's pollution and waste.

The range of environmental problems which threaten our planet are vast and their causes are equally diverse. But nearly all of them can be traced back to human activity, and to human consumption in particular. Use of the Earth's resources is necessary for survival, but the high consumption lifestyle enjoyed by most people in Canada and America depletes these resources faster than the Earth can renew them and creates waste and pollution faster than the Earth can absorb and process them. The above statistics demonstrate how a small proportion of the Earth's population is using the Earth's resources and services in a destructive and unfair manner. By overconsuming, not only do we hurt the Earth, but we also compromise the survival of our brothers and sisters on other parts of the planet.

One way to measure how our consumption patterns affect the Earth is through the Ecological Footprint. According to the Redefining Progress organization, the Ecological Footprint measures "the biologically productive area needed to produce the resources used and absorb the waste generated" by a population. A population can be a single individual, a community, a city, or an entire country. Divided equally between all the Earth's population, there are 1.88 global hectares (4.65 acres) of biologically productive land for each person. In 2004, the Canadian average Ecological Footprint was 8.56 global hectares (21.2 acres), and the American average was 9.57 global hectares (23.6 acres). If everyone in the world consumed at the same level as North Americans do, we would need two or three more planets. As a species, we are clearly exceeding the planet's capacity to sustain us and all the other creatures with which we share the Earth.

(Statistics from G. Tyler Miller, Sustaining the Earth, *5th ed. [Belmont, Calif.: Brooks/Cole Thomson Learning, 2002], 5; Redefining Progress, www.Redefining Progress.org)*

FOR DISCUSSION AND REFLECTION
What are some ways that you resist the culture of consumption?

faith connection

"Take care! Be on your guard against all kinds of greed; for one's life does not consist in the abundance of possessions."—Luke 12:15

When the Son of God came to Earth, he did not arrive with trumpets and red carpets and golden carriages. After his birth, he was laid in a manger—a feeding trough for animals—because there was no room in the inn, and he lived the rest of his life modestly and simply. Jesus's message about material possessions is unmistakably clear, both through his words and his actions: consumption and the accumulation of material wealth is not the way of God's kingdom. Instead, Jesus instructed his disciples not to be distracted by worrying about their material well-being. He even sent them off to preach and heal the sick without any provisions (Luke 9:3). Walking with Jesus really means walking! Adopting a simple lifestyle is a basic component of faithful stewardship.

FOR DISCUSSION AND REFLECTION

How do you sustain a spirituality of simplicity?

for meditation

"Consider the lilies, how they grow: they neither toil nor spin; yet I tell you, even Solomon in all his glory was not clothed like one of these. But if God so clothes the grass of the field, which is alive today and tomorrow is thrown into the oven, how much more will he clothe you—you of little faith! And do not keep striving for what you are to eat and what you are to drink, and do not keep worrying . . . Instead, strive for his kingdom, and these things will be given to you as well."—Luke 12:27-29, 31

for action

practice the 5 r's:

reverence, reduce, repair, reuse, recycle.

calculate your ecological footprint.

Basic test: www.mec.ca (go to About MEC—Social and Environmental Responsibility—Eco-footprint calculator) *In-depth test:* www.rprogress.org/ programs/sustainability/ef/

avoid disposable products such as razors and diapers.

Read Mary Jo Leddy, ***radical gratitude.*** Orbis Books, 2002.

for action

rent or borrow items you use infrequently.

avoid shopping for entertainment.

repair and mend damaged items.

Find other people who **share your values**; establish ways of supporting each other and keeping each other accountable in living simply.

Watch *affluenza*, a video available from MCC Resources (see online resource catalogue at www.mcc.org/respub.html).

avoid over-packaged items.

Look for products with the **EcoLogo** or other reliable labels that certify products as being less harmful to the environment. (See www.environmental-choice.com/ for Canada's official labelling program.)

WEEK 2
earth connection

After the September 11 terrorist attacks in 2001, President Bush's advice to the citizens of the United States to help stabilize their country was to go out and buy lots of stuff. Buying lots of stuff is a basic component of the market economy, which is the dominant economic system in the world today. This system is inspired by the ideas of a seventeenth-century economist named Adam Smith who argued that if everyone is free to pursue his or her own self-interests in the marketplace, an "invisible hand" will ensure that prices fairly reflect cost and that economic activity is equitable. Government interference (in the form of regulations, taxes, and subsidies) is frowned upon and competition is encouraged. Whether or not the invisible hand creates equity for people is debatable, but it is becoming increasingly clear that completely unrestrained markets have some grave consequences for the environment.

One of the most basic problems with the market system is the fact that environmental degradation is not accounted for in the pricing of goods. Without regulations, a business can pollute a river or destroy a forest without any obligation or motivation for replanting or remediation. Consumers then buy the products for less than they are actually worth because they are not paying for the environmental costs. When goods are cheap, consumers buy more and producers produce more, which then leads to even more environmental degradation. The emphasis on pursuing personal self-interest exacerbates this problem by encouraging individuals to think only about their own profit and gain.

Perhaps the most profound problem with today's economic system is the fixation on continual growth. The economy is perceived to be healthy if it is growing, but growth requires resources, and many of the Earth's resources are limited. One of the most basic physical laws is that neither energy nor matter can be created or destroyed. In such a universe, how can unlimited growth be sustained forever?

FOR DISCUSSION AND REFLECTION

How well do you think our economic system serves people and the Earth? How should it be changed?

faith connection

"But many who are first will be last, and the last will be first."—Mark 10:31

The prevailing wisdom of our culture instructs us to look out for "number one"— that is, ourselves—and to work hard to get ahead. But Jesus's life and ministry offer a different model of success, one which calls for humility and service. Grasping for more possessions, more prestige, and more power is presented as the surest way to lose everything (Matt. 6:19, Luke 14:7-11). Instead, we are called to be humble, to think first of God's kingdom and of others. The ultimate expression of this calling was given by Jesus in his willingness to give up his own life for the salvation of the world.

"Let the same mind be in you that was in Christ Jesus, who, though he was in the form of God, did not regard equality with God as something to be exploited, but emptied himself, taking the form of a slave, being born in human likeness. And being found in human form, he humbled himself and became obedient to the point of death—even death on a cross."—Philippians 2:5-8

FOR DISCUSSION AND REFLECTION

What brings true joy and fulfillment in your life?

for meditation

To live content with small means,
to seek elegance rather than luxury,
and refinement rather than fashion,
to be worthy, not respectable, and wealthy, not rich,
to study hard, think quietly, talk gently, act frankly,
to listen to stars and birds, babes and sages, with open heart,
to bear all cheerfully,
do all bravely,
await occasions,
hurry never—
in a word, to let the spiritual, unbidden, and unconscious,
grow up through the common.
This is to be my symphony.

—William Ellery Channing

Plan a
"buy nothing christmas"
(www.buynothingchristmas.org).
Encourage others
to join you.

donate
to and buy from second-
hand stores.

**for
action**

Buy products
built to last.

bring your own bags for shopping, especially at the grocery store.

buy locally manufactured goods and products—this reduces transportation impact and helps the local economy.

Hold a **garage sale**.

This week, **go through your closet**, garage or the storage room in your basement—set aside items you don't use and donate them to a second-hand store, a school or community centre.

make a list before you go shopping and only shop for what you need—shopping as recreation encourages unnecessary consumerism.

Carry a small notebook with you for one day. Every time you notice a message urging you to buy something, jot down where you were and the **source of the message**. At the end of the day, determine where you get the most messages urging you to buy. For one week, limit the messages you receive from that source.

During this week, **keep track of all the things that you buy**— do you really need everything that you purchase?

WEEK 3
earth connection

In 1928, a chemist named Thomas Midgely Jr., invented a miracle substance. He was searching for a refrigerant to replace the toxic gases that were being used at the time. These gases had caused fatal accidents when leaks occurred and posed a threat both to human health and to the environment. Midgely's miracle substance was called Freon and it was perfect in just about every way. It was odourless, colourless, nonflammable, noncorrosive, and nontoxic. Soon it was being used in all refrigerators, as well as in air-conditioners, aerosol cans, and plastic foam. Science and technology had triumphed again.

In 1973, however, traces of Freon (also known as chorofluorocarbons or CFCs) were found in the atmosphere and some scientists warned that when these gases reached the upper stratosphere, they would destroy the protective layer of ozone gases which shield the Earth from harmful solar radiation. By 1990, their theory was proven to be true and the countries of the world mobilized to phase out the production and use of these gases. CFCs were certainly an improvement to ammonia and methyl chloride as refrigerants, but like many technological innovations, their benefits were accompanied by unforeseen consequences.

Technology is both one of humanity's greatest accomplishments and one of our greatest enemies. Technology has assisted in many great human achievements from architecture, to music, to medicine, to space travel. It helps us attain our most basic needs and chase after our wildest fancies. It also gives us the power to profoundly alter our natural environment and has very often served as a tool of destruction. At the same time, technology can provide the innovation for more sustainable modes of working and living which can protect the environment.

Some people believe that it is not necessary to change our way of life or our attitudes toward nature because new technology will be developed to clean up all the messes we've already made and to prevent any future problems. But if the inappropriate application of technology has gotten us into the ecological situation we now face, can we depend on technology to get us out of it? As human beings, we cannot live without technology, but we must live very carefully with it.

FOR DISCUSSION AND REFLECTION
How much can we depend on technology to solve our environmental problems?

faith connection
In the biblical story, one of the greatest human temptations is to reject our creaturehood and to aspire to be like God. This tendency is manifested in the unrestrained applications of our technological innovations. The Tower of Babel is a classic example of this tendency: the people want to glorify themselves and strive to do so by the works of their hands. But they do not succeed because God confuses their language and they are scattered (Gen. 11:1-9). Because technology can become an instrument of sinfulness, its application must be evaluated carefully.

criteria for evaluating technology
- Is it sustainable? How well does it fit into the natural order?
- Does it promote justice? Is it beneficial to all society?
- What is its intent toward God? Is it a tool of faithfulness or sin?
- Does it provide creative and fulfilling work?

- What does it cost—economically, ecologically, socially, spiritually? Are these costs worth it?
- What are its long range effects?

(Adapted from S. Roy Kaufmann)

FOR DISCUSSION AND REFLECTION
Are technologies inherently good or bad, or are they morally neutral?

for meditation

"People cannot live apart from nature . . . And yet, people cannot live in nature without changing it. But this is true of all creatures; they depend upon nature, and they change it . . . But unlike other creatures, humans must make a choice as to the kind and scale of difference they make. If they choose to make too small a difference, they diminish their humanity. If they choose to make too great a difference, they diminish nature, and narrow their subsequent choices; ultimately, they diminish and destroy themselves. Nature, then, is not only our source, but also our limit and measure."
—*Wendell Berry*

for action

identify the five most important functions in your life that use technological labour-saving devices. How could these functions be done without technology or with simpler technology? What are the benefits and consequences of the technology you use? What are potential benefit for doing these things without technology or with simpler technology?

Go through your living space and garage (if you have one) and **identify gadgets that you never or rarely use**. Donate them to your local nonprofit re-use-it shop.

WEEK 4
earth connection

In 1999, the world human population reached 6 billion. Today, it is estimated at 6,314,000,000. Human populations have been increasing at exponential rates during the last 150 years. While population growth rates are now slowly beginning to decrease, the human population is in danger of overcoming the Earth's carrying capacity in coming decades.

The population size of any species correlates directly with its impact on the environment. Increases in the global human population magnify our Ecological Footprint as we require more land and resources, and produce more waste. Like consumption, however, human population growth is not consistent across the planet. Many countries in the global North, particularly in Europe, have zero or even negative growth rates, while countries in the global South tend to have burgeoning populations. Rapid population growth is directly related to economic welfare; higher birth rates almost always occur among low income populations. Having many children is a survival technique for the poor because children provide potential sources of income, old age security, and emotional fulfillment. In addition, where health care provision is poor and infant death rates are high, women have many children to ensure that some survive.

Discussions about environmental protection in the global North often focus on population issues as the major problem, which conveniently shifts the blame away from richer and more powerful societies. But we cannot evade our responsibility; it is still the consumption patterns of the wealthy nations that weigh most heavily on the Earth. There is also considerable evidence that the consumption patterns and economic activities of wealthy nations are responsible for the impoverishment of other countries. Consequently, addressing population problems requires a two-pronged approach: in the global South, it is necessary to reduce poverty, empower women through education and equal rights, and invest in family planning, while in the global North, fundamental changes in economic systems and consumption habits need to be made.

FOR DISCUSSION AND REFLECTION

To what degree is society justified in interfering with its members' reproductive behaviour? As the world becomes more overpopulated by humans, how do we decide who gets to live and reproduce, and who doesn't?

faith connection

"God blessed them and God said to them, 'Be fruitful and multiply, and fill the earth and subdue it; and have dominion over the fish of the sea and over the birds of the air and over every living thing that moves upon the earth."—Genesis 1:28

This passage has been used as a justification for the uncontrolled expansion of the human population and the abuse and desecration of the natural world. A careful reading of the passage with attention to the meanings of key Hebrew words and the context of early Hebrew culture conveys a very different message. The word which is usually translated as *multiply* can also be understood in terms of growing in wisdom and sensitivity. The word translated as *fill* connotes gift-giving, while the word for *subdue* describes putting weight on something in the way that one would knead bread. Based on these distinctions, a better translation might go as follows:

"Be fruitful and mature, grow in wisdom and sensitivity, bring a gift to the earth, rub the earth tenderly and make it function properly so that the fish, and the sea, and the birds, and the air, and the animals, and the forests, and the lakes, rivers, and streams, and all people will continue to become good."
(Adapted from Robert Salzgeber)

FOR DISCUSSION AND REFLECTION

Having children is often understood by Christians as an act of hope and faithfulness to God. In the context of a ballooning human population, what are faithful and responsible options for Christians wishing to start a family?

for meditation

Great Spirit,
give us hearts to understand;
never to take from creation's beauty
more than we give;
never to destroy wantonly
for the furtherance of greed;
never to refuse to give our hands
for the building of earth's beauty;
never to take from her
what we cannot use.

Give us hearts to understand
that to destroy earth's music
is to create confusion;
that to wreck her appearance
is to blind ourselves to beauty;
that to callously pollute her fragrance
is to make a house of stench;
that as we care for her
she will care for us. AMEN.

—U.N. Environmental Sabbath

**consider
population issues**
when you plan
to have a family of
your own.

**for
action**

Support
organizations that
provide programs and
funding for **family planning** (eg. United Nations
Fund for Population
Activities).

Write
to your elected
representative to voice
your support for foreign aid
for **education and
employment for women**
in the global South.

WEEK 5
earth connection

One of the more harmful consequences of the European colonization of South America was the establishment of a highly inequitable system for the distribution of land. This has resulted in widespread poverty and continues to pose significant obstacles to development in many countries.

During the 1950s and 1960s, the Brazilian government tried to address this situation by providing land for settlement to the landless people filling the slums and barrios of its cities. After all, there were enormous tracts of unsettled land in the rainforest which were simply waiting to be filled. "Land without people for people without land" was the promotional slogan. With help from international organizations like the World Bank, the Brazilian government began building highways through the Amazon.

As roads opened up the wilderness, people came, cleared the forest and began farming. But the rainforest is not suited for agriculture, and after several years of cultivation, the soil became depleted of nutrients and the crops failed. The farmers were faced with the choice of either starving or clearing more forest and starting again . . . and again . . . and again. By the late 1990s, Brazil was losing two million hectares of rainforest every year. While poverty is not the only cause of rainforest destruction, it is a very significant factor.

In today's world, almost one of every four people lives in poverty. These 1.4 billion people are unable to meet their basic needs. This is a disgrace for all of humanity, and is also an enormous threat to the health of the Earth. People who live in desperate poverty struggle each day to find food, fuel, and a source of income, and they cannot think about the future costs of overcultivating their land or cutting down too many trees. Desperation often forces them to use resources in unsustainable ways. Sadly, this in turn often makes them more vulnerable to droughts, floods, and other natural disasters, which impoverish them further. At a national level, governments of poor countries will reduce their environmental standards in the hope of attracting foreign investment. Many of the cheap goods which citizens of the global North enjoy were manufactured at great cost to the environment in sweat shops in the global South. World poverty is a problem which hurts all of creation.

FOR DISCUSSION AND REFLECTION

What are other examples of the connection between poverty and environmental degradation?

faith connection

A young man who had kept all the commandments since his youth asked Jesus what else he should do to inherit eternal life.

"Jesus looked at him, loved him, and said, 'You lack one thing; go sell what you own, and give the money to the poor, and you will have treasure in heaven, then come, follow me.'"—Mark 10:21

Concern for the underprivileged and the oppressed has been a fundamental responsibility of God's people since the beginning (Deut. 15:4). The psalmist praises God's redemption of the poor while the prophets invoke judgment on oppressors (Isa. 10:1-4; Amos 5:11-12). Concern for the poor is also a dominant theme in the Gospels. Mary foresees the lifting up of the lowly and the hungry being filled with good things (Luke 1:52-53). Jesus starts his ministry by announcing: "The Spirit of the Lord is upon me, because he has anointed me to bring good news to the poor. He has sent me to proclaim release to the captives and recovery of sight to the blind, to let the oppressed go free, to proclaim the year of the Lord's favor" (Luke 4:18). In the world today, both the Earth and the poor are crying out. We must not forget about one in our zeal to help the other.

FOR DISCUSSION AND REFLECTION
In his book, *Cry of the Earth, Cry of the Poor*, Brazilian theologian Leonardo Boff argues that the root cause of both poverty and the ecological crisis is "the ongoing disruption of the basic connectedness with the whole of the universe and with its Creator that the human being has introduced, fueled, and perpetuated." How do you respond to this statement?

for meditation
a prayer of healing
We join with the earth and with each other.

To bring new life to the land
To restore the waters
To refresh the air

We join with the earth and with each other.

To renew the forests
To care for the plants
To protect the creatures

We join with the earth and with each other.

To celebrate the seas
To rejoice in the sunlight
To sing the song of the stars

We join with the earth and with each other.

To recreate the human community
To promote justice and peace
To remember our children

We join with the earth and with each other.

We join together as many and diverse expressions of one loving mystery:
for the healing of the
earth and the renewal of all life.

—U.N. Environmental Sabbath Program

for action

Encourage your government to **increase its foreign aid** to poorer countries to the UN-recommended level of 0.7 percent of GDP.

Support the **cancellation of international debt** owed by poorer countries.

Become **globally informed**.

"Think globally, **act locally**."

Participate in an **exchange program** with a country from a different economic level or do a service assignment.

Buy **fair trade** coffee, tea, and chocolate (MCC's Ten Thousand Villages stores sell fair trade items).

buy clothing that is not made in sweat shops.

educate yourself about where products you buy are made and who makes them.

WEEK 6
earth connection

"The city is not an ecological monstrosity. It is rather the place where both the problems and the opportunities of modern technological civilization are most potent and visible."—Peter Self

Today 50 percent of the world's population lives in urban centres. Unfortunately, few cities are sustainable systems. They require an immense input of energy and resources from outside sources and produce massive amounts of waste, pollution, noise, and heat which must be absorbed by the surrounding environment. These problems are magnified when cities begin to sprawl with the growth of low-density suburbs around their periphery. Sprawling neighbourhoods with big houses, big lawns, and lots of roadways waste valuable crop land, forest, grassland, and wildlife habitat. Sprawl also increases motor vehicle usage, which causes pollution. In the global South, where cities are growing the most rapidly, many of these problems are compounded by a lack of economic resources, resulting in poor housing, water treatment, waste disposal, and pollution controls.

Cities can be ecological monstrosities, but they don't have to be. Curitiba, Brazil, is an example of how creativity and innovation can make a city into a pleasant and sustainable place to live. It is a city designed for people, with plenty of pedestrian zones, the world's best bus system, and lots of trees and parks. The industrial zone is located downwind from the rest of the city and is controlled by strict air and water pollution control laws. While Curitiba has not been able to avoid the growth of slums, the plague of all Brazilian cities, its slums are cleaner and better maintained than most. Garbage in these areas is cared for by a program through which residents receive food in exchange for bringing garbage to collection sites. The quality of life in Curitiba is higher than in other Brazilian cities and probably higher than in many North American cities as well. This has been achieved by caring for the natural world rather than degrading it.

FOR DISCUSSION AND REFLECTION

What are your favourite aspects of the city in which you live (or the city nearest your home)? What are things you would like to see improved?

faith connection

The book of Revelation illustrates the story of sin and salvation as it pertains to both people and creation in evocative terms. The book is pervaded by dark visions of how human greed and excess cause the absolute collapse of the natural world. The fallen city of Babylon is the representative symbol of this decay (Rev. 18). In response to human sinfulness, God employs nature, in the form of volcanoes, storms, hail, and fire, as the instrument of judgment on humans, but the Earth is also punished in the process. Throughout the turmoil and chaos, however, the faithfulness of God, the Creator and Redeemer, is remembered. And ultimately, when the terror and destruction have run their course, the Earth is restored and made whole again.

It is of great significance that God's response to the evils of Babylon is not a return to Eden, the idyllic garden of the original creation. Instead, in the re-creation of the world, God builds the new Jerusalem, a holy city which houses both the tree and the water of life. The creating power of God and the redeeming recreation of salvation are active at all times and in all forms of human society.

FOR DISCUSSION AND REFLECTION

What is your vision of renewal for the Earth and human society within it?

for meditation

"Then I saw a new heaven and a new earth; for the first heaven and the first earth had passed away, and the sea was no more. And I saw the holy city, the new Jerusalem, coming down out of heaven from God, prepared as a bride adorned for her husband . . . Then the angel showed me the river of the water of life, bright as crystal, flowing from the throne of God and of the Lamb through the middle of the street of the city. On either side of the river, is the tree of life with its twelve kinds of fruit, producing its fruit each month; and the leaves of the tree are for the healing of the nations. Nothing accursed will be found there any more. But the throne of God and of the Lamb will be in it, and his servants will worship him; they will see his face, and his name will be on their fore-heads. And there will be no more night; they need no light of lamp or sun, for the Lord God will be their light, and they will reign forever and ever."—Revelation 21:1-2; 22:1-5

for action

If you live in a city, **take a walk** through your neighbourhood. What aspects of your urban environment promote sustainability? What aspects promote over-consumption?

Find out if your city has an **environmental policy** or vision (city Web sites usually contain this information). Is your city living up to its own standards? Write a letter to your city councillor to voice your support for improvements towards sustainability.

are caring for the environment and maintaining a healthy economy incompatible goals?

I think it depends on your definition of a "healthy economy." I would consider it fairly incompatible with the standard definition our society uses. But I have to ask, is an economy that in large part relies on exploiting people and nonrenewable resources, while disregarding and impairing natural ecosystems, and encouraging a pattern of ever increasing consumption and waste, really a healthy one in anything but economic terms?

If we redefine a healthy economy as one that can be maintained indefinitely on a finite planet, then I think caring for the environment would not only be compatible, it would be a key component of it. Such an economy would seek to meet needs in a sustainable way, and not have growth as its primary goal.

— *7-Days trek participant*

unbashed praise

When one stifles joy or retreats from commitment, part of our soul withers. The lid is kept firmly battened down and while nothing gets in to do damage, nothing gets out to express the great cosmic wonder of it all.

At church, it is such an absolute relief to unabashedly sing and praise and let the joy course through my entire body. There is so little praiseworthy these days, my entire being rejoices and is refreshed by worship and song.

— *7-Days trek participant*

the hallowed rest . . .

Day 7: **the hallowed rest**

"Everybody needs beauty as well as bread, places to play in and pray in, where nature may heal and give strength to body and soul."—John Muir

On the seventh day, God rested, and so on the seventh "day" of this trek, we will explore the idea of rest, both in terms of the faith implications of Sabbath-keeping and in terms of the practical issues relating to rest and recreation in the natural places of our planet.

"Thus the heavens and the earth were finished, and all their multitude. And on the seventh day God finished the work that he had done, and he rested on the seventh day from all the work that he had done. So God blessed the seventh day and hallowed it, because on it God rested from all the work that he had done in creation."—Genesis 2:1-3

WEEK 1
earth connection

In 1883, three railway workers surveying the eastern Rocky Mountains stumbled upon natural hot springs in a cave at the base of a mountain. This discovery led to the creation of Canada's first national park, and today, Banff is one of the most popular tourist destinations in the country. A decade earlier, the first national park in the world had been created in the U.S. at Yellowstone. These groundbreaking events set a precedent for conservation around the world, as people realized that areas with exceptional natural beauty and uniqueness need to be set aside and preserved. Today there are more than 102,000 national parks, wilderness reserves, heritage sites, and other protected areas worldwide, encompassing more than 18.8 million square kilometers.

The goal of the parks system in Canada is to preserve representative natural areas for public understanding, appreciation, and enjoyment in the present and for future generations. The difficulty in fulfilling such a mandate is to find the right balance between public access and preservation. Often the very success of a park may spell its ruin as millions of visitors flock to enjoy its attractions.

benefits of parks and conservation areas
- storage and discharge of water
- purification of the air
- generation of topsoil
- habitat for important species, such as the insects that pollinate our crops
- storehouses of biodiversity for food and medicines
- economic benefits through tourism and jobs
- cultural and spiritual benefits.

challenges in parks and conservation areas

- overcrowding resulting in traffic jams, pollution, litter, crime, and vandalism
- resource violations, such as collecting plants, illegal logging, and poaching
- development around and within park borders which creates pollution, breaks ecosystems into small fragmented pieces, and creates obstacles for migration
- decline in government funding and support
- decline in the populations of some species, especially bears, wolves, and other carnivores
- overproliferation of other species, especially elk, which overgraze and can pose a danger to tourists
- invasion of exotic species which threaten indigenous species and disrupt natural habitats.

solutions

- suppress car traffic and create alternative public transportation options
- create super-parks and green corridors which connect parks together, linking fragmented ecosystems
- collaborate with neighbouring communities
- ensure that park staff have sufficient resources to care for protected areas
- address global climate change
- coordinate global efforts through international initiatives like the U.N. Convention on Biological Diversity. The United States has not yet signed this agreement.

FOR DISCUSSION AND REFLECTION

What is your favourite park or wilderness area? What makes it special?

faith connection

On the seventh day, the day which God hallowed, God rested. Many of the activities which lead to environmental destruction are motivated by the urge to do more, be more, make more, have more. The imagination and drive which human beings possess are things that make our species unique, but the Sabbath reminds us to pause for a moment and experience the world exactly as it is. We can appreciate its inherent wonder and beauty without any effort and thereby gain a better understanding of the Creator—and perhaps also gain wisdom about how to better apply our own creative and active energies. The Sabbath rest enables us to be fully immersed in the joy and beauty of the created world.

FOR DISCUSSION AND REFLECTION

Do you think that humans need beauty to thrive? How do you fulfill this need in your life?

for meditation

"Beauty, like peace, is our soul's birthright. We nourish ourselves in the deepest way when we make and share beauty. Beauty provides inspiration as well as sanctuary. It helps us attune to that place of deep inner peace at our core. It encourages balance and serenity.

"When beauty is connected to nature and to nature's cycles of life, it is even more compelling. Then we are reminded of our place in the universe and of the natural harmony of all creation."—Louise Diamond

for action

Set aside a few minutes every day to go for a walk in your neighbourhood and **notice the wildlife**.

Go birdwatching or **explore wild places** near you.

Purchase a **field guide** on trees, wild flowers, insects, or animals and learn to identify different species in the wild.

find out where the nearest park or wilderness area is near you. What challenges does it face and what can you do to help?

start an environmental group or committee at your church to promote creation care education discussion and action; integrate creation care into Sunday school curricula and worship service or set up a study group on ecology in your church.

Set up a bird or **butterfly feeder** in your yard or on your balcony.

Decorate your home, office, and church with objects which **remind you of God's creation**, such as rocks, stones, feathers, leaves, and flowers. (If you pick wild flowers, be sure to take only the very common ones.)

WEEK 2
earth connection

Deep in the Bolivian jungle, in the middle of Madidi National Park, the fortunate visitors to the Chalalan Ecolodge can experience a close encounter with the rainforest with the assurance that their visit is benefiting all parts of the community. While staying in traditional cabañas built from sustainably harvested rainforest materials, guests can take guided hikes and canoe trips, and view birds and wildlife. The Chalalan Ecolodge is a model of community-based ecotourism. The lodge is owned and run by the Quechua-Tacana community of San Jose de Uchupiamonas. Conservation International and the Inter-American Development Bank provided initial funding and training for the villagers, who now operate it independently. The income from the project has enabled the village to acquire radio and telephone service and a new middle school, while preserving the forest and its flamboyant flora and fauna. Without the lodge, the villagers would be forced either to leave the village or to log the forest to support themselves. Instead, the community members can enjoy the natural heritage of their home—the howler monkeys, butterflies, and three-toed sloths—while benefiting from luxuries like the satellite dish that connects them with the outside world.

Ecotourism is a form of travel which supports the local people while promoting environmental conservation and sustainable resource use. When executed well, it is a most effective tool for long-term biodiversity conservation. Ecotourism enterprises are popping up all over the world, from the Amazon to South Africa, providing opportunities for many people to gain economic autonomy and to share their knowledge and love for their land. This trend should be celebrated cautiously, however, because not all ecotourism initiatives are as successful in meeting their goals as the Chalalan Ecolodge. An influx of visitors can wreak devastation on a fragile environment or community, and responsible tourists need to be keenly aware of the impacts their presence may have on both the people and the land. But despite ongoing struggles to fine-tune the industry, ecotourism is still a cause for celebration because it stands as a shining beacon of hope for a world in which people can make a living and live gently on the Earth at the same time.

faith connection

The Sabbath is a reminder of grace. The Earth has been given to its creatures as a gift; it is not conditional on whether or not we are deserving of it. Grace permits us to pause in our frantic efforts to fix all that has been damaged to enjoy the gift of the Earth, and to remember what it is that we are working for and why. Grace also leads us to thanksgiving. Living life in a state of constant gratitude— for the gift of the Earth and for life itself—connects us to creation in a profound way and becomes the greatest gift that we can give back to the Earth and to the Creator.

FOR DISCUSSION AND REFLECTION

What are things that you receive without payment from your family, friends, society, the Earth, and from God? What are things that you give "for free" to family members, friends, and those in need? Do these lists feel "balanced" or "unbalanced"?

for meditation

O give thanks to the Lord, for he is good,
  for his steadfast love endures forever.
O give thanks to the God of gods,
  for his steadfast love endures forever.
O give thanks to the Lord of lords,
  for his steadfast love endures forever.

who alone does great wonders,
  for his steadfast love endures forever;
who by understanding made the heavens,
  for his steadfast love endures forever;
who spread out the earth on the waters,
  for his steadfast love endures forever;
who made the great lights,
  for his steadfast love endures forever;
the sun to rule over the day,
  for his steadfast love endures forever;
the moon and stars to rule over the night,
  for his steadfast love endures forever ...

...O give thanks to the God of heaven,
  for his steadfast love endures forever.

—Psalm 136:1-9, 26

for action

practice thankfulness rituals, like saying grace at each meal.

celebrate the Earth's bounty by sharing with others.

This week, **make an offering to the earth,** in the form of a prayer or some other gift.

**enjoy
non-motorized
outdoor activities:**
canoeing, sailing, windsurfing,
hiking, camping in summer; skiing, skating, snowshoeing
in winter.

**when you visit
wilderness areas,**
avoid picking plants or feeding animals, and take away with
you everything you
brought in.

**create a nature
sanctuary** in your yard
or home with house plants
or outdoor plants or bird feeders, to be a place where you can
rest and remember the
beauty and gift
of creation.

feeding a deep hunger
Being outside after dark when the stars are bright lifts me "out of myself." That
is restful. I hung an upside down finch feeder outside the kitchen window this
spring. Being within two feet of a gorgeous American Goldfinch makes me feel I
am being given a gift every time they grace the feeder. And then there are
babies—human babies, newly-hatched chicks, and tadpoles. All of them feed a
deep hunger. I think they give me hope.— *7-Days trek participant*

**acknowledgments
& bibliography**

acknowledgments

I would like to recognize the contributions of Esther Epp-Tiessen, coordinator of MCC Canada's Peace Ministries program, who originally conceived of this project and provided valuable guidance throughout the process. I would also like to thank Carol Thiessen, who gave me excellent editorial advice in the early stages of writing.

I used a large number of quotations, the sources for which are listed below according to chapter. Sources for older materials that are in the public domain have not been included in this list.

introduction
McFague, Sallie. *Super, Natural Christians: How We Should Love Nature.* Minneapolis: Fortress Press, 1997.

in the beginning . . .
Amish Prayer, quoted in Redekop, Calvin, ed. *Creation and the Environment: An Anabaptist Perspective on a Sustainable World.* Baltimore: Johns Hopkins University Press, 2000.

"Evangelical declaration on the care of creation." *Creation Care* 9 (Spring 2000).

Heschel, Abraham, quoted in *The EarthCare Toolkit: An Ecumenical Resource for Christian Churches.* Edited by Margaret Cameron, Carole Christopher,

Elaina Hyde-Mills. Burnaby, B.C.: A Publication of the Earth Justice Project of The Jubilee Community for Justice & Peace, 1991.

Leopold, Aldo. *A Sand County Almanac: With Essays on Conservation from Round River.* New York: Ballantine Books, 1959.

van Geest, William. *God's Earthkeepers: Biblical Action and Reflection on the Environment.* The Evangelical Fellowship of Canada, 1995.

Day 1: **let there be light . . .**
Ellis, Havelock, quoted in Meyer, Art and Jocele. *Earthkeepers: Environmental Perspectives on Hunger, Poverty and Injustice.* Scottdale, Pa.: Herald Press, 1991.

Gerlach, Barbara A. *The Things That Make for Peace.* New York: Pilgrim Press, 1981.

Day 2: **the blue planet . . .**
Eckhart, Meister, quoted in *The EarthCare Toolkit: An Ecumenical Resource for Christian Churches.* Edited by Margaret Cameron, Carole Christopher, Elaina Hyde-Mills. Burnaby, B.C.: A Publication of the Earth Justice Project of The Jubilee Community for Justice & Peace, 1991.

Todd, John, quoted in Miller, G. Tyler. *Sustaining the Earth*, 5th ed. Belmont, Calif.: Brooks/Cole Thomson Learning, 2002.

Day 3: **the holy earth . . .**

Carson, Rachel. *Silent Spring*. Boston: Houghton Mifflin, 1962.

Julian of Norwich. http://conservation.catholic.org/prayers_ii.htm

Kaufman, S. Roy. "Preaching on Environmental Concerns: Obstacles and Themes for Taking Ecology Seriously in the Church." Seminar presented at Mennonite World Conference, Winnipeg, Manitoba, July 25, 1990.

Lowdermilk, Dr. C. W., quoted in Redekop, Calvin, ed. *Creation and the Environment: An Anabaptist Perspective on a Sustainable World.* Baltimore: Johns Hopkins University Press, 2000.

The North American Conference on Christianity and Ecology, quoted in *The EarthCare Toolkit: An Ecumenical Resource for Christian Churches.* Edited by Margaret Cameron, Carole Christopher, Elaina Hyde-Mills. Burnaby, B.C.: A Publication of the Earth Justice Project of The Jubilee Community for Justice & Peace, 1991.

U.N. Environmental Sabbath, quoted in *The EarthCare Toolkit*.

Day 4: **gambling with the sun . . .**

Black Elk, quoted in Rowthorn, Anne W. *Caring for Creation: Toward an Ethic of Responsibility.* Wilton, Conn.: Morehouse Publishing, 1989.

Colinvaux, Paul A., quoted in Miller, G. Tyler. *Sustaining the Earth*, 5th ed. Belmont, Calif.: Brooks/Cole Thomson Learning, 2002.

David Suzuki Foundation. "Declaration of Interdependence." www.davidsuzuki.org/About_us/Declaration_of_Interdependence.asp

Kaza, Stephanie, from Roberts, Elizabeth and Elias Amidon, eds. *Earth Prayers: From Around the World, 365 Prayers, Poems, and Invocations for Honoring the Earth*. San Francisco: HarperSanFrancisco, 1991.

Rowthorn, Anne W. *Caring for Creation*.

St. Francis. "Canticle of the Sun." www.conservation.catholic.org/prayers.htm.

Day 5: **all creatures . . .**

deChardin, Teilhard, quoted in McCarthy, Scott. *Celebrating the Earth: An Earth-Centered Theology of Worship with Blessings, Prayers and Rituals*. San Jose, Calif.: Resource Publications, Inc., 1991.

Leopold, Aldo Leopold. *A Sand County Almanac: With Essays on Conservation from Round River*. New York: Ballantine Books, 1966.

Zerbe, Gordon. *Creation, Environment and the Bible*. Class taught at Canadian Mennonite University, Winnipeg, Man., 2000.

ACKNOWLEDGMENTS

Day 6: **in God's image . . .**

Berry, Thomas. *The Great Work: Our Way into the Future.* New York: Bell Tower, 1999.

Berry, Wendell. *Home Economics.* San Francisco: North Point Press, 1987.

Kaufmann, S. Roy. "Preaching on Environmental Concerns: Obstacles and Themes for Taking Ecology Seriously in the Church" and "Technology and Nature: What Kind of Difference Should Humans Make in the Natural World?" Seminars presented at Mennonite World Conference, Winnipeg, 1990.

Salzgeber, Robert. *Second Mile* Student Pamphlet, Pathway A, Creation Care 3. Scottdale, Pa.: Faith & Life Resources.

Self, Peter, quoted in Miller, G. Tyler. *Sustaining the Earth*, 5th ed. Belmont, Calif.: Brooks/Cole Thomson Learning, 2002.

U.N. Environmental Sabbath, quoted in *The EarthCare Toolkit: An Ecumenical Resource for Christian Churches.* Edited by Margaret Cameron, Carole Christopher, Elaina Hyde-Mills. Burnaby, B.C.: A Publication of the Earth Justice Project of The Jubilee Community for Justice & Peace, 1991.

U.N. Environmental Sabbath Program, *UNEP Environmental Sabbath/Earth Rest Day Kit,* 1989.

Day 7: **the hallowed rest . . .**

Diamond, Louise. *The Peace Book: 108 Simple Ways to Create a More Peaceful World.* Berkeley, Calif.: Conari Press, 2001.

bibliography

resources

MCC Resources and Publications (in particular, the Environment listings in the
MCC Resource Catalogue). www.mcc.org

Schrock-Shenk, David, ed. *Basic trek: Venture into a World of Enough*. Scottdale,
Pa.: Herald Press, 2002.

bible study and worship resources

Crisfield, Erin. *God's People, God's Planet: Living Lightly on the Earth*. Toronto,
Ont.: The Presbyterian Church in Canada, 2001.

The EarthCare Toolkit: An Ecumenical Resource for Christian Churches. Edited by
Margaret Cameron, Carole Christopher, Elaina Hyde-Mills. Burnaby, B.C.:
A Publication of the Earth Justice Project of The Jubilee Community for
Justice & Peace, 1991.

Jubilee Celebrations #3, Session #7 "Working in the Garden." Scottdale, Pa.: Faith
& Life Resources, 1996. (1-800-743-2482)

McCarthy, Scott. *Celebrating the Earth: An Earth-Centered Theology of Worship with
Blessings, Prayers and Rituals*. San Jose, Calif.: Resource Publications, Inc,
1991.

Roberts, Elizabeth and Elias Amidon, eds. *Earth Prayers: From Around the World, 365 Prayers, Poems, and Invocations for Honoring the Earth.* San Francisco: HarperSanFrancisco, 1991.

Second Mile: A Peace Journey for Congregations. Edited by Carol Penner. Scottdale, Pa.: Faith & Life Resources. (See Pathway A, Creation Care. 1-888-743-2482)

van Geest, William. *God's Earthkeepers: Biblical Action and Reflection on the Environment.* The Evangelical Fellowship of Canada, 1995. (905-479-5805)

White, Vera K. *It's God's World: Christians, Care for Creation and Global Warming.* Elkhart, Ind.: The Eco-Justice Working Group, National Council of Churches of Christ in the USA, 2002.

christian environmental books

Berry, Thomas. *The Great Work: Our Way into the Future.* New York: Bell Tower, 1999.

Berry, Wendell. *Home Economics.* San Francisco: North Point Press, 1987.

Berry, Wendell. *What Are People For?* San Francisco: North Point Press, 1989.

Boff, Leonardo. *Cry of the Earth, Cry of the Poor.* Maryknoll, N.Y.: Orbis, 1997.

DeWitt, C., ed. *The Environment and the Christian: What Can We Learn from the New Testament?* Grand Rapids: Baker, 1991.

Fox, Matthew. *The Coming of the Cosmic Christ*. San Francisco: Harper & Row, 1988.

Granberg-Michaelson, Wesley. *Tending the Garden: Essays on the Gospel and the Earth*. Grand Rapids: Eerdmans, 1987.

Hall, Douglas John. *The Steward: A Biblical Symbol Come of Age*. Rev. ed. New York: Friendship Press, 1989.

Hallman, David, ed. *Ecotheology: Voices from the South and the North*. Maryknoll, N.Y.: Orbis Books, 1994.

Lehman, Donna. *What on Earth Can You Do? Making Your Church a Creation Awareness Center*. Scottdale, Pa.: Herald Press, 1993.

Longacre, Doris Jantzen. *Living More with Less*. Scottdale, Pa.: Herald Press, 1980.

Mcfague, Sallie. *Super, Natural Christians: How We Should Love Nature*. Minneapolis: Fortress Publishers, 1997.

Meyer, Art and Jocele. *Earthkeepers: Environmental Perspectives on Hunger, Poverty and Injustice*. Scottdale, Pa.: Herald Press, 1991.

Redekop, Calvin, ed. *Creation and the Environment: An Anabaptist Perspective on a Sustainable World*. Baltimore: Johns Hopkins University Press, 2000.

White, Lynn Jr. "The Historical Roots of Our Ecological Crisis." *Science* 155 (1967): 1203-7.

Young, Richard A. *Healing the Earth : A Theocentric Perspective on Environmental Problems and Their Solutions.* Nashville: Broadman, 1994.

christian environmental periodicals

Creation Care, a Christian environmental quarterly, available from Evangelical Environmental Network, 10 E. Lancaster Ave., Wynnewood, PA 19096-3495; 1-800-650-6600; www.esa-online.org/een

Earthlight, magazine on spiritual ecology, available from 111 Fairmount Ave., Oakland, CA 94611.

Earth Letter, available from Earth Ministry, 1305 NE 47th Street, Seattle, WA 98105, (206) 632-2426.

social and ecological books

Adams, Douglas and Mark Carwardine. *Last Chance to See.* London: Pan Books, 1990.

Alvord, Katie. *Divorce Your Car!: Ending the Love Affair with the Automobile.* Gabriola Island, B.C.: New Society Publishers, 2000.

Carson, Rachel. *Silent Spring.* Boston: Houghton Mifflin, 1962.

Durning, Alan. *How Much is Enough? The Consumer Society and the Future of the Earth.* New York: W. W. Norton & Co, 1992.

Leopold, Aldo. *A Sand County Almanac: With Essays on Conservation from Round River.* New York: Ballantine Books, 1966.

McKibben, Bill. *Hope, Human and Wild: True Stories of Living Lightly on the Earth.* Boston: Little, Brown, 1995.

Suzuki, David and Holly Dressel. *Good News for a Change: Hope for a Troubled Planet.* Toronto: Stoddart, 2002.

Suzuki, David and Amanda McConnell. *The Sacred Balance: Rediscovering Our Place in Nature.* Vancouver: Greystone Books, 1997.

Wackernagel, Mathis and William Rees. *Our Ecological Footprint: Reducing Human Impact on the Earth.* Gabriola Island: New Society Publishers, 1996.

children's books

Cooney, Barbara. *Miss Rumphius.* New York: Viking Press, 1982.

Cherry, Lynne. *The Great Kapok Tree: A Tale of the Amazon Rain Forest.* San Diego: Harcourt Brace Jovanovich, 1990.

Dr. Seuss. *The Lorax.* New York: Random House, 1971.

Hamm, Wes. *God's Great Outdoors: Faith Building Family Activities.* Scottdale, PA: Faith & Life Press, 2000.

Horsfall, Jacqueline. *Play Lightly on the Earth: Nature Activities for Children 3 to 9 Years Old.* Nevada City, Calif.: Dawn Publications, 1997.

Wood, Douglas and Cheng-Khee Chee. *Old Turtle.* New York: Scholastic Inc, 1992.

christian web sites

indicates sites with worship and/or Bible study resources

A Rocha * www.arocha.org

Arbor Vitae www.arborvitae.org

Au Sable Institute of Environmental Studies www.ausable.org

Catholic Conservation Center * conservation.catholic.org/index.htm

Christians in Science www.cis.org.uk

Earth Ministry * www.earthministry.org

Earthlight: The magazine of spiritual ecology * www.earthlight.org

Evangelical Environmental Network * www.creationcare.org

European Christian Environmental Network * www.ecen.org

The John Ray Initiative * www.jri.org.uk

Kairos www.kairoscanada.org

National Council for Churches Eco-Justice Working Group *
www.webofcreation.org/ncc/index.html

National Religious Partnership for the Environment www.nrpe.org

Target Earth—Serving Earth, Serving the Poor www.targetearth.org

The US Conference of Catholic Bishops Environmental Justice Program
www.nccbuscc.org/sdwp/ejp/index.htm

advocacy group web sites
Adbusters www.adbusters.org

Canadian Environmental Network www.cen-rce.org

Council of Canadians www.canadians.org

David Suzuki Foundation www.davidsuzuki.org

The Earth Charter Initiative www.earthcharter.org

Environmental News Network www.enn.com

Friends of the Earth www.foe.org

Global Resource Action Centre for the Environment www.gracelinks.org

Greenpeace www.greenpeace.ca

The Sierra Club www.sierraclub.ca

consumer information web sites

Arbour Environmental Shoppe www.arbourshop.com

Eat Well Guide www.eatwellguide.org

Energy Star www.energystar.gov

Environmental Choice Program www.environmentalchoice.com

Real Goods www.realgoods.com

government and research web sites

Environment Canada www.ec.gc.ca

International Institute for Sustainable Development www.iisd.org

United Nations Environment Programme www.unep.org

U.S. Environmental Protection Agency www.epa.gov

World Resource Institute www.wri.org

The Worldwatch Institute www.worldwatch.org

about the author

Joanne Moyer has degrees in theology from Canadian Mennonite University and in environmental studies from the University of Winnipeg. She has been a research assistant for Agriculture Canada and the University of Winnipeg, and a research consultant for Panterra Management, a Winnipeg environmental consulting firm. Most recently she served as the research writer for Mennonite Central Committee's web site on creation care. Moyer is currently pursuing a masters degree in environmental studies at Dalhousie University in Halifax, Nova Scotia. She is a member of Lethbridge Mennonite Church in Alberta.

What to do when enough is enough

Basic trek
Venturing into a World of Enough
"The point of our Christian faith is not that we have less than we need, but that everyone has enough. A simple idea . . . enough for everyone. Enough food, clothes, recreation. Enough time with family. Enough quietness. Enough time with God. But what is enough? *Basic trek* is a four-week guide to help you explore this question. Includes daily reflections, discussion questions, and suggested activities. An ideal resource for youth groups, young adult groups, and small groups." —*MCC Resource Catalog*
Paper, 96 pages, 0-8361-9215-X: U.S. $10.99; Can. $15.49

Parent trek
Nurturing creativity and care in our children
"This innovative parenting resource shares ways to raise creative, generous, and joyful children. Follows the rhythms of life with children: school, play, relationships, and faith. Each of the 12 chapters includes a meditation, personal experiences, reflection questions, and practical ideas to try."
 —*MCC Resource Catalog*
Paper, 192 pages, 0-8361-9193-5: U.S. $11.99; Can. $16.79

Herald Press

Mennonite Central Committee (MCC) is a relief, service, and peace agency of the Mennonite and Brethren in Christ churches of Canada and the United States. MCC has some 1,500 workers serving in fifty countries in food production, health, education, job creation, refugee assistance and peacemaking.

Mennonite Central Committee <www.mcc.org>
21 South 12th St, PO Box 500, Akron, PA 17501-0500 USA; (717) 859-1151 or toll free (888) 563-4676
134 Plaza Drive, Winnipeg, MB R3T 5K9 CANADA; (204) 261-6381 or toll free (888) 622-6337